GARLAND STUDIES ON INDUSTRIAL PRODUCTIVITY

edited by
STUART BRUCHEY
UNIVERSITY OF MAINE

A GARLAND SERIES

REORGANIZING WORK

The Evolution of Work Changes in the Japanese and Swedish Automobile Industries

BEN SACHS

GARLAND PUBLISHING, Inc.
New York & London / 1994

Library of Congress Cataloging-in-Publication Data

Sachs, Ben, 1971–
    Reorganizing work : the evolution of work changes in the Japanese
and Swedish automobile industries / Ben Sachs.
        p.   cm. — (Garland studies on industrial productivity)
    Includes bibliographical references and index.
    ISBN 0–8153–1641–0 (alk. paper)
    1. Automobile industry and trade—Japan—Case studies.
2. Automobile industry and trade—Sweden—Case studies.
3. Industrial productivity—Japan—Case studies.   4. Industrial
productivity—Sweden—Case studies.   I. Title.   II. Series.
HD9710.J32S23   1994
338.6—dc20   93–42756
                                                               CIP

Printed on acid-free, 250-year-life paper
Manufactured in the United States of America

Contents

Preface

This is a book about the effects that differing organizations of work in the automobile industry have on the workers that labor according to their dictates. Within the context of the crisis of Fordism, industry is scrambling to find new ways to organize production in order to compete successfully in post-Fordist markets. While the Japanese model of work organization, as exemplified by Toyota, seems to be the answer to the production questions posed by Fordism's demise, this work system has severe implications for Toyota workers, and for the workers laboring in factories modeled after this system. Through a comparative study of Toyota and Volvo, this book argues that there is more than one post-Fordist work organization, and that Volvo's answer to the crisis of Fordism—as exemplified by its Uddevalla plant—had far more positive implications for workers than does Toyota's.

This book does not attempt to study the productivity of the two systems. However, I do not address this topic without any regard for productivity. What good is an auto plant with a humanized work system, for example, that cannot survive in real markets? At the time of the original writing of this manuscript, Volvo's Uddevalla plant was still in operation. In fact, at that time, Uddevalla's productivity rates were increasing and its quality index improving. But on May 9, 1993 the Uddevalla plant was closed. This closing does not pose a direct challenge to the thesis of this book: regardless of Uddevalla's closure, the conditions which led to the development of the plant and the implications that the work system employed there had on the work force—the issues to which this study addresses itself—remain the same.

Yet, the plant's closing does raise an important question: Can a work system as revolutionary as Uddevalla's, one which rehumanizes and professionalizes auto work, realistically survive in post-Fordist markets? Thanks to recent research done by Christian Berggren, we can begin to answer this question. Berggren points out that according to an October 1992 study, Uddevalla was Volvo's "best practice plant," placing ahead of the Gothenburg operation which remains open following Uddevalla's closure. Uddevalla reached Gothenburg's productivity level as early as 1991, and by November 1992 Uddevalla

was producing cars at 39 hours/car while Gothenburg was taking 42 hours. Uddevalla also bettered Gothenburg in terms of quality.

Berggren also points out that Uddevalla's ability to produce directly to customer orders made it ideal for post-Fordist markets. By November of 1992, 70% of the cars produced at Uddevalla were built specifically to customer order, while at Gothenburg only 30% were built to order. Uddevalla had also cut lead time in half—from 60 to 30 days—in one year! By standard measures, Uddevalla *was* meeting the demands of post-Fordist markets.

Why, then, did Volvo choose to close Uddevalla? Volvo asserts that the depressed conditions of the auto market demanded closing the plant. Indeed between 1989 and 1992 Volvo sales of large cars dropped 30%, raising questions of over-capacity for Volvo. But why Uddevalla? Berggren argues that corporate politics had a lot to do with the decision. Renault, a major shareholder of Volvo, opposed Uddevalla, in Berggren's words, as an "aberration and abnormality for these ardent adherents of large-scale plants and authoritarian management." But Renault, apparently, came to this opposition having "never bothered to study Uddevalla's performance."[1] Sören Gyll, the new Volvo CEO, also favored the closing because of the benefits he saw in consolidating production. As perhaps the unkindest cut of all, moreover, the Metall union *favored* the closing as a means to save jobs at the Gothenburg plant.

While the actual reasons for the closing may remain partly unclear, it seems clear that Uddevalla was shut more in spite of productivity considerations than because of them. Berggren argues that Volvo's slow product development was the "real problem," and thus the small flexible nature of Uddevalla's production system would be ideal for correcting Volvo's plunging sales. In any case, the fact that Uddevalla did outpace the more traditionally organized Gothenburg facility inclines us to see Uddevalla, despite its closing, as a viable alternative to the Toyota model. That Uddevalla is a preferable alternative in terms of the implications of the work system for the post-Fordist work force will be demonstrated below.

NOTES

1. Christian Berggren, *Volvo Uddevalla—a dream plant for dealers?* (Stockholm: Royal Institute of Technology Department of Work Science, February 1993).

Introduction

In the United States, during the post-World War II era, an economic order designed to solve the problems posed by the Great Depression and to facilitate an industrial sector dominated by mass-production firms was developed. To this end, a series of institutions evolved which incorporated the state, organized labor, and business into the functioning of the economy. In order to stabilize the mass demand necessary to solve the crisis of underconsumption—exposed by the Depression—and to support mass production of standardized goods, unions bargained collective wage contracts ensuring that wages expanded in line with productivity growth, and states provided welfare provisions and full-employment policies. Collectively, these institutions made up a "regime of accumulation" known as Fordism, or the Fordist economic order, which will be detailed in Chapter One. On the level of the macropolitical economy, Fordism was designed to ensure stabilized mass markets; on the microlevel of the shop floor, the Fordist system of work organization facilitated production of the mass quantities of standardized goods which these markets demanded.

This Fordist organization of the shop floor was, therefore, economically rational only within a specific political economy, and by the early 1970s this political-economic context was facing a crisis. The stability of mass markets, which had allowed economic growth based on standardized mass production, was crumbling. The institutions that had ensured stability during the 1950s and 1960s began to induce *de*stabilization by the early 1970s, while several exogenous factors, including the oil shock of 1973, also contributed to increasing economic instability. With the Fordist macropolitical-economic context in decay, the Fordist organization of work was decreasingly able to ensure either productivity or competitiveness for America's industrial firms. Moreover, during the late 1960s and early 1970s, the Fordist organization of work, across Europe and the U.S., came under attack from another source—those workers who had labored according to its dictates. In the context of destabilized markets, the evolving post-Fordist economy, and increasingly vocal labor protests, the search for a "new" system of work organization has been intense.

The primary inspiration for this book derives from the recent obsession among American business with the Japanese model of work organization. Especially for firms in the automobile sector—where Fordism's crisis and the search for alternative forms of work organization have been especially intense—the Japanese system is heralded as the solution to the fundamental problems posed by the crisis of Fordism. First, because the Japanese model of organizing work provides a flexible production system, it is seen as the key to successful competition in post-Fordist international markets. Second, in solving the problems that have plagued the auto industry for the past 15 years, many claim that the Japanese system of work organization also humanizes the nature of production work: workers in "team concept" plants are said to have new opportunities in the work process, new degrees of control over their work, as well as the opportunity to work in greatly improved factories.

According to many in American business circles the Japanese model of work organization is *the* answer to the crisis of Fordism. Through a comparative study of work organization systems in the Japanese and Swedish automobile industries, however, this book attempts to demonstrate that the Japanese model is but *one* alternative to Fordist production methods, and that there are other systems of work organization which are equally capable of achieving the flexibility demanded by post-Fordist markets. Perhaps more importantly, I argue that these alternatives to Fordist work organization have very different implications for the post-Fordist work force.

To this end, I endeavor to do three broad things. First, I ask how the two national industries, which both sought to provide flexible production through a reorganization of work, developed such different systems of work organization. By way of answering this question, I argue these work changes developed not only in response to economic conditions which demanded the capacity for flexible production, but as a result of the *interaction* between these economic conditions and the strength of organized labor—supported or discouraged by the state— in each nation.

The reorganization of work in both countries was a response to this interaction, but the historical contexts were significantly different in Japan and Sweden. In the Japanese case, the reorganization of work came in the early 1950s in response to non-Fordist economic conditions, including demand for a diversified product line and small domestic markets, which forced flexibility on the Japanese automakers. Thus, the Japanese model, while solving the economic challenges that would eventually be posed by post-Fordism, did not evolve in response

to Fordism's crisis. The changes in the Swedish auto industry, however, did come in response to the crisis of Fordism, and attempted to address the economic challenges of post-Fordism. Again, however, the alternative systems of work organization do not only reflect the demands of these non-Fordist economic contexts. Rather, as I attempt to show, the work changes in Japan resulted from the interaction between the economic demand for flexibility and a *weak and defeated* labor movement, while the changes in Sweden came as a result of the post-Fordist demand for flexibility and a *highly organized and powerful* social democratic labor movement.

Having seen the factors that led to the work changes in Japan and Sweden, and understanding that the nature of these changes, while delimited by the economic context is determined by a broader mix of forces, I go on to describe, and deconstruct, the systems of work organization at Toyota and Volvo. Through these case studies the above claims are borne out. That is, the organization of work at Toyota is flexible in a way that addresses management's desire for flexibility, but that does not address the implications of the work system for the work force. In contrast, the organization of work at Volvo is flexible in a way that incorporates union demands for the humanization of work and for increased worker power and autonomy.

Finally, I describe the implications of the two work systems for the Toyota and Volvo workers. As might be expected, though contrary to the claims made recently, Toyota has achieved production flexibility through a system of work organization defined by the continuous intensification of work, complete managerial control over the work process and the deployment of the labor force, and an institutionalized regime of peer pressure. The nature of the work process has also forbidden worker identification with the completed product, and has eliminated worker power resources vis-a-vis management by deskilling all jobs and appropriating worker knowledge of shop-floor production processes. In contrast, Volvo, having been forced to incorporate a union voice, has developed flexibility through a shop-floor organization wherein work is less fragmented, less standardized, and more skilled than work in a traditional Fordist plant. Additionally, the Volvo system extends autonomy and control to the work force, and facilitates the integration of mental and manual labor.

The argument is presented according to the following progression. In Chapter One, I develop an ideal-type model of the Fordist economic order. In this model I address both the macro elements of Fordism—collective wage bargaining, the role of the state, the international

economy, etc.—as well as the Fordist organization of work on the shop floor. I also attempt to show how this organization of the shop floor only makes economic sense within the macro Fordist economy. In Chapter Two, I present an ideal-type description of the crisis of Fordism. Here I explain not only the breakdown of Fordism's macro institutions, but the effect of this collapse on the Fordist organization of work. In Chapter Three, I argue that the preconditions for the work changes in the Japanese auto industry resulted from the conjunction of specific economic demands of the 1950s and the defeat of the Japanese labor movement, which led to the development of ineffectual enterprise unions. Likewise, in Chapter Four I argue that the development of the work organization changes in the Swedish auto industry came as a result of both the economic demands of the post-Fordist international economy and the strength of the Social Democratic labor movement. Chapters Five and Six are comparative case studies of the Japanese and Swedish auto industries. In Chapter Five, I describe Toyota's system of work organization, and in Chapter Six I describe Volvo's. In both chapters I discuss the impact of the systems of work organization on workers.

In the conclusion, I discuss the implications of this study for the future of work in the American auto industry. If, contrary to the opinion widely held in American business circles, there is more than one alternative to the Fordist organization of work, American auto firms and American auto unions are faced with a decision regarding the way in which they adapt to Fordism's crisis. For the auto companies, this implies a reevaluation of the "team" work systems they are now implementing, while for the unions, the evidence presented in this book implies that survival in post-Fordist markets is not dependent on labor's submission to managerial conceptions of flexibility. On the contrary, what this book suggests is that a form of flexibility, which enhances the quality of work life as well as labor's power and autonomy on the shop floor, may be secured through the strength of American labor, and the vocalization of demands by American auto unions.

Acknowledgments

This book benefited greatly from the advice and constructive comments of Professor Chris Howell, my thesis advisor at Oberlin College. Professor Howell's courses formed the core of my career at Oberlin and I owe him my sincerest thanks. I would also like to express my gratitude to Professor Marc Blecher who not only served as my second thesis reader, but who has been a mentor for the past four years. I am additionally grateful to Claudia Hirsch at Garland Publishing for all of her help. Gabrielle Gallucci provided me indispensable support during the original writing of this manuscript at Oberlin, and assisted in the preparation of the final manuscript. To her I am sincerely thankful. Finally, I extend my deepest thanks to Murray, Merle, and Jonathan Sachs.

I would like to acknowledge the financial support provided by the Harry S. Truman Scholarship Foundation, and to extend thanks for the following publication permissions. *The Evolution of Labor Relations in Japan: Heavy Industry 1853-1955* by Andrew Gordon, and *The Japanese Automobile Industry* by Michael Cusumano reprinted by permission of Harvard University Press, Cambridge, Mass.: Harvard University Press, Copyright 1985 by the President and Fellows of Harvard College; *Reforming Industrial Work* by Kajsa Ellegård, Tomas Engström, and Lennart Nilsson reprinted by permission of The Swedish Work Environment Fund and the authors (The Swedish Work Environment Fund finances research and development, education and information to promote a better work environment);*The Golden Age of Capitalism* by Andrew Glyn, Alan Hughes, Alain Lipietz, and Ajit Singh reprinted by permission of Oxford University Press, Oxford, England: Oxford University Press, Copyright 1990; "Radicalism and Retreat in Swedish Social Democracy" by Jonas Pontusson, and "Third World Industrialization: 'Global Fordism' or a New Model?" by Alice Amsden reprinted by permission of New Left Review, London, England: New Left Review, 1987 and 1990; *Politics in Hard Times* by Peter Gourevitch reprinted by permission of Cornell University Press, Ithaca, New York: Cornell University Press, 1986; *The Second Industrial Divide* by Michael Piore and Charles Sabel reprinted by

Reorganizing Work

Chapter One
The Fordist Economic Order

In order to understand the recent developments in the world automobile industry, it is necessary to look at the broad phases, or "regimes of accumulation," of the advanced capitalist economy that provided the political-economic context for these changes in production. Through an investigation of the era of Fordism (roughly 1950-1973) and the crisis that dismantled this regime of growth and production (roughly 1973-present) the current interest in new forms of flexible work organization makes sense. Furthermore, by investigating Fordism, the nature of the pressures that led the Japanese and Swedish auto industries to reorganize work in the ways that they did becomes clear.

On the level of the macro-political economy the ideal-type model of the Fordist economy incorporates the broad compromises made between business, labor, and the state which facilitated rapid growth of national economies. Primary to these relationships were the various mechanisms developed to balance supply and demand, mainly through state Keynesian demand management policies and through the collective bargaining of wages between business and labor unions. Crucial to the success of these demand maintenance mechanisms in securing a high growth economy was the primacy of the domestic economy in the typical Fordist nation. I also develop an ideal type model of the Fordist system of work organization: based on mass production of standardized goods, work in the Fordist firm was organized around the flow of a mechanized assembly line, and was defined by high degrees of standardization and regimentation. Finally, this chapter looks at the relationship between the macro components of Fordism and the micro system of work organizations they supported.

Developing this ideal-type model of the Fordist nation and the Fordist firm will provide a sense of the shared features of advanced capitalist economies during the post-World War II years, and will help clarify the national divergences from the typical Fordism. Moreover, understanding Fordism, both on the level of the macro-political

economy and on the level of the shop floor, will make clearer the reasons for the crisis which brought down these systems in the mid-1970s.

1. MACRO-FORDISM

Henry Ford and the Great Depression

The economic growth that took place following World War II was born out of the crisis and chaos of the Great Depression. The institutions and mechanisms established in the advanced capitalist countries during the postwar era were thus designed to respond to the failures in the free market system which the Depression had brought to light, and to provide a context in which the evolving systems of mass production could flourish. Although there were multiple causes of the Depression, and while banking failures and the stock market crash may have initiated the Depression, it was, above all else, a crisis of underconsumption—a crisis of demand—which led to the downward spiral of the economy.

Throughout the interwar period, with the help of new forms of work organization—including Taylorite organizations of labor—and new machines—particularly specialized machine tools used in conjunction with the automated assembly line—industry had become increasingly productive: the interwar period saw the birth of mass production of standardized products. The problem with the economy was that supply increased at a rate far beyond the rate of increase of purchasing power. This severe mismatch of supply and demand resulted in a fall in profit margins, and as a result wages were cut and investments abandoned. Wage and investment cuts further diminished demand, and a downward cycle ensued. The result was severe economic depression.

Henry Ford developed the mass production factory—in response to the crisis of underconsumption—which gave a name to the postwar period. In 1913, at the Ford plant in Highland Park, Michigan, Ford introduced the automobile assembly line and production levels of the Model-T, Ford's only car model at the time, took off. While the introduction of the mechanized serial flow line led to great increases in productivity, the assembly line itself was the culmination of a series of work process rationalizations, the standardization of product, routinization of production, and employment of specialized machine

tools, all of which contributed to the fantastic increases in production levels.[1] Nonetheless, Ford himself was plagued by the same mismatch of supply and demand that caused the Depression: Ford was producing cars at incredible rates, but there weren't enough people with the consumption power to buy them all.

In response to this dilemma and others (including high labor turnover), Ford began paying his workers $5 a day with the belief that this wage would enable them to buy the cars they built. The problem that Ford ran into quite quickly, however, was that there was nothing to ensure that his workers would buy Ford cars instead of Chryslers, or instead of any other goods. Acting alone, the Ford company's solution to the crisis of demand would not work. Somehow demand and production had to be matched on a national scale, and the stability of these markets, once established, had to be protected.

The situation that Ford faced, writ large and with numerous intricacies drawn in, would come to define the economies of the advanced capitalist nations in the post-World War II years. Production was to be standardized, routinized, and given over increasingly to very expensive specialized machines so that it could become faster and cheaper. In order to compensate for the huge investments made in this specialized machinery, production runs were to be very long, resulting in the production of huge quantities of standard items. To ensure demand for these mass-produced items, consumption levels were to keep pace through wages with the booming increases in productivity.

Compromise and Stabilization

Peter Gourevitch, in his book *Politics in Hard Times*, argues that as a result of these developments, after World War II there was a cross-national striving for stabilization. He writes of a common seeking for a "stabilization model . . . to contain the chaos to which capitalism was vulnerable," a chaos evidenced by the Depression.[2] Labor had revolted against the market across all of the advanced capitalist nations, as a result of the privations brought on by the Depression. The critical, and *new*, element in the postwar era, however, was the desire on the part of business to restrict some of the operations of the free market, and to develop some mechanisms to ensure the existence of sufficient demand, and to stabilize this demand. This shift in business ideology and strategy was a result of the new dominance in industry of mass-production firms. It was the demands of an industry that depended on continually expanding and stable mass markets, an industry that was forced to invest in specialized machinery and long production runs,

which led business to embrace the development of demand management and market stabilization mechanisms. In fact, all of the developments that arose in these years were designed basically to address this relationship: mass production requires stabilized mass markets.

As both labor and business were thus interested in managing the workings of the market, they were in a position to compromise. As Gourevitch writes:

> Labor movements . . . abandoned, or least put on hold, their aspirations for extensive socialization of the economy. In exchange they got the welfare state, collective bargaining, and acceptance into the political system. Business abandoned, or least put on hold, desires for a passive labor force so atomized that workers could be treated as a pure commodity, and accepted much of the welfare state and considerable government participation in economic management. In return they got an acceptance of private ownership, the primacy of profits and the market, rejection of planning and complete nationalization, and free trade and strong currencies.[3]

On the micro level of the firm, as will be discussed below, the compromise entailed a trade-off of high and rising wages in exchange for labor's acceptance of boring and repetitive tasks, *and managerial control over investment and production*.[4] In other words, high wages, including a high social wage, were exchanged for labor peace. The state, moreover, played a crucial role in facilitating this compromise by providing welfare and full-employment policies.

These components made up, in one form or another, the typical compromise between business, labor, and the state in the postwar era. Collectively they assured growth by providing two things: demand and stability.

Collective Wage Bargaining

Wage growth was the first means by which the mass demand which sustained and expanded an economy based on mass production was provided. As Andrew Glyn et al. point out in *The Golden Age of Capitalism*, firms began to balance growth in productivity with growth in real wages. In order to ensure that consumption levels kept pace with productivity increases, collective wage bargaining by unions was

employed. As Piore and Sabel write, "The centerpiece of the postwar macroeconomic stabilization was the system of national wage determination that resulted from the rise of trade unions in mass-production industries and the concomitant spread of collective bargaining."[5] With unions and firms bargaining high and rising wages, the growth of real wages in tandem with the growth in productivity ensured that there would be markets of mass demand able to absorb the mass production of goods. This equation was critical for the success and growth of the economy.

It should be noted that the success of national demand stabilization mechanisms in the Fordist economy was predicated on the primacy of domestic markets. According to Glyn et al., the export share of GDP in the U.S. in 1950 was 4.3%, and in the OECD as a whole exports were 10.3% of GDP. This reflects the limited extent to which trade and foreign markets were a factor in sustaining demand. By way of comparison, in 1984, export's share of GDP had doubled, reaching 8.2% in the U.S., and 21.3% in the OECD as a whole.[6] Because of this domestic focus of the Fordist economic system, rising wages were not likely to lead to an increase in imports, but rather to an increase in demand for domestically produced goods.[7]

The tandem growth of wages and productivity not only provided sufficient domestic demand, however, it also ensured the stability of this demand. Indexation of wages and productivity, another result of union-management bargaining, enabled investors to forecast relatively well the rate of growth of consumption.[8] Investments in costly specialized machinery which called for long production runs and huge initial capital outlays could be made with relative confidence. This existence of investment security was another key ingredient of Fordist growth. With productivity, wages, and investment all growing together, there existed the potential for a "virtuous circle" of growth: as productivity rates rose (as a result of new machinery, new forms of work organization, etc...), wages rose as well. With rising wages came increased demand for industrial goods; thus profits increased for industry, and in this context of economic stability, new investments were made, which led to increases in productivity, which led to higher wages, and so on. While this circle was operant, both business and labor benefited, and the Fordist compromise remained workable.

The processes through which such collective bargaining was carried out varied across countries, but the basic system of wage determination was typical across the Fordist era. In general, leading companies or business federations reached collective agreements with representatives of workers, and these agreements subsequently set the standard wages

for that firm or industry. Typically, the formula for setting these wages would incorporate increases in labor productivity and the change in the consumer price index. That is, wages would grow in accordance with increases in productivity, as well as with increases in the cost of living. Typically, then, wages became indexed to prices through collectively bargained cost-of-living adjustments (COLAs). Once a wage agreement was reached, it was spread, either by law or union pressure to other firms or industries within the national economy. Thus, as Piore and Sabel put it:

> Given that labor productivity adjusted for price changes is a measure of productive capacity, consistent and uniform application of the formula to all wages and salaries would ensure that private-consumer purchasing power would expand at the same rate as national productive capacity.[9]

It is important to note that this model of wage determination was labor inclusive; it not only legitimized but required union existence, strength, and involvement in the economy. Yet the acceptance of this form of bargaining by business was predicated on the need to match wages and productivity, not on business's acceptance of a strong labor movement. More subtly, this form of bargaining was predicated on the need to equate wages and consumption. That is, in any market economy, demand is always needed to meet supply. It is in a mass-production economy, however, that this demand comes primarily from the working class and thus from industrial wages. Only in such a situation will this type of wage determination make sense to business. In a polarized economy where a small upper class is responsible for sustaining economic growth through purchasing a smaller but more expensive set of luxury goods, the Fordist model of labor inclusive collective bargaining will no longer seem economically rational to business. Wages in such a polarized economy are likely to be perceived only as a cost to business, and much less as a component of demand.[10] Business acceptance of union involvement in collective wage bargaining thus rests on the existence of a mass-production/mass-consumption regime of accumulation.

While this wage structure worked to ensure steady economic growth, it also posed the threat of inflation. As discussed earlier, wages in the Fordist era were tied to productivity increases and indexed to prices, which assured that if wages kept pace with productivity and prices, demand would be maintained and stabilized. However, if wages

grew faster than increases in productivity, a spiral of inflation could result because wages were the major component of costs. As prices rise, wages will rise again setting off a further price increase, and the cycle keeps repeating. Inflation, especially this type of cyclical inflation, has disastrous implications for market stability. The future contours of industrial markets become increasingly difficult to predict, and thus long-term investments—those central to a mass production economy— become increasingly tenuous. As, Piore and Sabel write, "The viability of the whole system thus depended on institutional mechanisms to forestall unsettling price increases."[11] During the postwar boom years when the Fordist system was running smoothly, such wage increases were preventable, thanks in part to the presence of large labor reserves which guaranteed labor at the prevailing wage. However, the elimination of these reserves, along with increasing labor militancy, among other things, threatened to destroy this balance.

The longer-term solution, which proved more difficult to achieve, was the development of corporatism within the Fordist nations. The unions agreed not to use their market power to harm the economy in exchange for inclusion in corporatist bargaining structures that determined national wage rates and shaped the contours of the national economy, in addition to state provision of welfare and full-employment policies. Primarily, the corporatist unions had to agree to some measure of wage restraint in order to avert these potentially disastrous inflationary spirals. Corporatist bargaining also worked to ensure labor peace by providing a non-strike alternative for expression of union demands. This labor peace formed another element of the stability of the Fordist model.

The Role of the State: Keynesianism, Welfare Policies and Full-Employment

Thus a particular structure of wage bargaining developed during the Fordist era which, while vulnerable, managed to balance production and consumption and to stabilize demand markets enough to facilitate the long range investments necessary for mass production. Wages, however, were not the only mechanism that supplied the requisite demand and stability for the sustenance of this Fordist economy. The state also had a role to play. In the mass-production economy, individual corporations and their products were ultimately dependent on the prosperity of the national economy in which they were located. Just as Henry Ford's $5 day wasn't enough to secure demand for Ford automobiles, collectively bargained wage increases alone weren't able to

secure demand and stability for corporations operating on the national level.

The argument for a state role in demand maintenance came from economist John Maynard Keynes. Keynes argued that private market economies are prone to fall into an "underconsumption trap" wherein there is not sufficient demand to support high levels of production; as a result output falls, and there is no mechanism to restore production to its previous level.[12] In order to escape this "trap," Keynes argued that government spending should be employed to act as demand stimulus, a strategy that was followed, to greater or lesser extents, in the advanced capitalist countries.[13]

A major element in Keynesian demand management came through state provision of economic support for economically underprivileged individuals and families. Welfare provisions including unemployment insurance, collective provision of health care, family allowances, etc., all served to provide consumption power to those who otherwise would have been unable to contribute any demand to the economy. The state also stepped in to provide jobs for the unemployed through public works projects and to sustain wage levels through mandatory minimum wage laws. In Europe, the proportion of GDP devoted to such transfers and subsidies rose from 8% in 1955-1957 to about 12% in the late 1960s and to about 16% by the mid-1970s. Likewise, income maintenance rose from 8.3% of GDP in 1962 to 11.4% in 1972.[14]

Moreover, just as wage bargaining provided market stability as well as demand, the new Keynesian state policies worked to stabilize Fordist markets. The increased levels of total government spending were financed largely by taxation, and this increased level of taxation amounted to what Glyn et al. refer to as the "increased fiscal leverage" of the state. This "leverage" was used by national governments to stabilize markets through counter-cyclical management. That is, in times of economic boom which threatened inflation, the government could cut spending or raise taxes, which would decrease demand and put downward pressure on prices. Further, if the economy began to slump, the government could further increase spending, or cut taxes, and in either case stimulate demand. While this could, and did, lead to government deficits during slumps in the business cycle, these deficits acted as buffers against market instability. Through acquiring deficits, the government compensated for slack in the market until the economy picked up again. Thus "public expenditures directly fostered and reinforced expectations of high and stable demand."[15] Again, this stability was critical for an economic order based on a production

strategy that required investments in costly specialized machinery and long production runs.

Beyond stabilization through this fiscal leverage, many of the state welfare provisions developed during the Fordist era acted as "automatic stabilizers." For example, unemployment insurance provides a de facto wage for those out of work. In doing so, unemployment insurance provides consumption power for those who would otherwise be unable to purchase anything. In a booming economy there are few people out of work, and thus government expenditures on unemployment insurance are low. As an economy slows and more people are forced out of work, government spending on unemployment insurance rises automatically. Thus decreases in demand due to slumps in the business cycle are automatically offset (to some extent) by increased government spending. Again, state involvement in the economy served to stabilize markets in the Fordist era. Gourevitch sums up this element of Fordism when he writes, "Welfare programs helped not only recipients but producers, providing a floor to demand and a stabilizer for the swings of the open market."[16]

The typical Fordist state also played a role in stabilizing demand through the development of full-employment policies. While there were wide variations across countries, the typical policy involved some sort of commitment on the part of the state to ensuring that unemployment did not rise above a determined level. To this end, states provided active labor market and training programs designed to facilitate the transfer of unemployed workers from one job to another as quickly as possible, as well as state-funded works projects. Such policies worked to ensure not only full-employment, but the stability of consumption levels that went along with low levels of unemployment. Full-employment policies also encouraged the development of corporatist bargaining structures and, thereby, wage restraint (see above), and by tightening labor markets, these policies strengthened the unions (see Chapter Two).

One final role the state played in supporting the Fordist economy came in the realm of investment. As we've seen, part of the "virtuous circle" of Fordist growth was the high level of investment, especially in new machinery that could improve labor productivity. In order to facilitate this level of investment, the states in advanced capitalist economies in the postwar years acted to keep interest rates low. Costello argues that these "easy credit" policies underpinned the postwar boom.[17]

The International Economic Order

While both wages and the state were used to solve the major problems of the Fordist era—demand and stability—an international economic order, developed during the Fordist era, worked along with wages and states to solve these problems. As established in the mid-1940s at Bretton Woods, there were two main elements of the international context in which Fordist economies operated. The first was a set of institutions established to ensure stability: the International Monetary Fund (IMF) functioned as the international organization for the maintenance of exchange stability, and the International Bank for Reconstruction and Development (IBRD) was the organization established to deal with long-term international investment.[18] In order to become a member of the IMF, countries had to peg their currencies to gold or to the U.S. dollar, which was convertible into gold. Revaluation or devaluation of currency was basically prohibited and was allowed only in unusual circumstances with the IMF's approval. While these policies may have restricted maneuverability in domestic economic policy, by fixing exchange rates they created a stable international economy where financial markets were predictable. Again, predictability, this time on an international scale, was crucial in an economy where long-term investment decisions were necessary.

Yet the Fordist international order was not simply designed to be stable, it was also designed to ensure growth. Such growth in international trade was to be assured by the liberalization of trade regulations. This was secured through the General Agreement on Trades and Tariffs (GATT). Members of the GATT agreed to create no barriers to trade other than tariffs and agreed that over time the level of tariffs would be reduced. By opening up international trading markets, markets that could consume mass-produced goods were extended, which indeed contributed to the expansion of trade during the postwar years.[19]

These then were the institutions established to extend demand and ensure stability on an international level. In maintaining the Fordist international economy, however, the American economy was perhaps equally important as these institutions. The Bretton Woods exchange rate agreements, as shown above, were predicated on member nations' willingness to hold their reserves in dollars and to settle international accounts with dollar payments. The United States was able to fulfill its role as provider of the medium of international exchange due to its unique position following World War II—its was the only economy left intact after the war. As a result, the other advanced capitalist countries were dependent on the U.S. for their reconstruction, and thus the U.S.

became the capitalist world's international creditor. The demand for dollars, which was the corollary to this relationship, sustained an international economic and financial order based on the U.S. dollar.

2. MICRO-FORDISM

While the above summarizes the central elements of Fordism as a macroeconomic phenomenon, this definition of Fordism excludes the heart of the regime—the organization of production and the system of shop-floor relations. To complete this explanation of the Fordist economic order, it is thus necessary to present an ideal-type model of the Fordist shop floor.

The Organization of Work

As noted above, the Fordist production system was based, above all else, on the manufacture of mass-produced standardized products. In this respect, the postwar era was very much an extension of the interwar years. The logic behind the adoption of mass-production techniques hinged largely on reaping the benefits of economies of scale. The logic behind the manufacture of standardized products was slightly more complex. First, and most obviously, in order to manufacture products on a mass scale, the introduction of machinery and the substitution of this machinery for the human worker was necessary. No craft workers could produce the number of widgets that a widget machine could produce. But while humans can vary their labor to vary the products they manufacture, the specialized machines available at this time were not able to do so. Thus, because of the dictates of the technology used in mass-production factories, a technology chosen according to the demands of mass production, all of the component parts of manufactured products, and therefore the products themselves, had to be standardized.[20] It is important to note, moreover, that in order to compensate for the large investment in the specialized machines, very long production runs were needed.

With mass production of standardized products came a system of work organization that was also largely extended from the prewar days. The primary tenet of this system of work organization came from Adam Smith himself. Smith argued that efficient production (the highest possible output per unit of effort) was dependent upon the division of labor. In his classic example, taken from *The Wealth of Nations*, Smith

argues that a top-of-the-pin maker and a bottom-of-the-pin maker will make more pins in a given period of time than two whole-pin makers. With this impetus, work was organized in such a way that each production worker would perform one simple task. Manufacture of a given product, then, involved the combination of a series of simple tasks performed by a group of workers rather than the manufacture of a complete product by any one worker.

While Smith's contribution was certainly significant, the production efficiency goal was furthered by Frederick W. Taylor. Taylor agreed that the division of labor was crucial for production efficiency, but believed that a "scientific" analysis of production techniques was necessary in order to establish the "one best way" for workers to carry out their assigned tasks. Thus, following the infamous time-and-motion studies, all production workers within a given firm would be instructed exactly how to carry out their tasks and how much time they were to spend on each repetition of the task. In this way, work within the mass-production factory became standardized—each worker had one task to complete, and this task was rigidly defined by the "scientific" managers. This development was tied to the decision to produce standardized products for mass markets.

During the early postwar years, the standardization of tasks was incorporated into the machinery itself. While in Taylor's day managers would design the one best way to carry out a task and instruct production workers to follow this model, with the introduction of specialized machines in the postwar years, tasks were defined by the dictates of producing with the machines. Because the machines could do only one thing, and could do it in only one way, workers had little or no choice as to how to carry out their tasks.[21]

A further component of the Fordist system of work organization, which was also a contribution of Taylor, was the separation of conception and execution of work, or in Marx's terminology, the division between mental and manual labor. In the Taylorist factory, all decisions regarding the nature of the products to be produced and the way in which they were to be produced, were made by a core of engineers and managers removed from the shop floor. Production workers were to have no role in these decisions; they were responsible only for carrying out their standardized tasks. In the Fordist era this division of conception and execution of work was reinforced by the introduction of specialized machines. Incorporating machines into production meant that the organization of work was largely dictated by technicians who built these machines and the managers who determined how the machines were to be incorporated into the work process.

Production workers, having a say in neither the design of the machines nor the way in which the machines were incorporated into the work process, were denied any voice in the organization of their work. With the introduction of the assembly line, moreover, the entire production process, not only its component parts, became dictated by the pace and flow of a mechanized belt. There was no longer any room for creative input from the workers involved in production. As Kaplinsky put it, "Detailed production workers are seen as thoughtless commodities; like foot-soldiers, their job is to follow orders and the dictates of the machine rather than to exercise any initiative or creativity."[22]

Implications for Management and Workers

The cumulative effect of the division of labor, the standardization of tasks, and the division of conception and execution of work was to facilitate the use of unskilled labor by industrial employers. Craft production, where one worker is responsible for the manufacture of a completed product, requires that workers have skills. By dividing labor into simple, standardized tasks and by assigning all mental labor to managers, production workers no longer needed skills. For management this was a very attractive development: unskilled labor is much cheaper than skilled labor, and unskilled workers do not have the power that accompanies the possession of a skill.

The implications of this form of work organization on production workers, however, were very different and much more deleterious. The detailed division of labor and standardization of tasks led to a deskilling of work and of the work force. While this may have improved efficiency, it amounted to a destruction of what had once been meaningful work for production workers. The loss of skill amounted to a loss of workers' power vis-a-vis management, and made workers interchangeable. Therefore they could not withhold their skills as a means of securing their demands. Furthermore, workers were no longer involved in the manufacture of any complete product. The new form of work organization forced them to produce only components of products that were completed later. This alienated each worker from the products in which they invested their labor, and thereby detracted from the meaning and satisfaction of work.

The nature of production work represented an attack on the quality of life of production workers, as each worker was required to engage in repetitive and boring work all day long, repeating without variance the same simple task hundreds or thousands of times every day. Over the course of a working lifetime, the mental and physical strain of such

work was significant. Furthermore, the severe separation instituted between mental and manual labor denied production workers the use of their creative and intellectual faculties in their work. Indeed, managers and the work organization itself actively discouraged such creativity: human workers were to be unthinking adjuncts to the specialized machinery and the assembly lines that now dominated mass-production factories.

Implications for Unions

The Fordist system also had an impact on the role that unions played on the shop floor, stemming from the typical Fordist compromise. In return for high wages, inclusion in collective bargaining, an extensive welfare state, etc., unions ceded to management the right to manage. All production, investment, and work organization decisions were securely in the hands of managers and were not at issue in labor-management relations. Therefore, in a context defined by strict and narrow job definitions, Fordist unions on the shop floor struggled mainly over task classifications and job rules, and developed restrictive job definitions which enabled unions to secure a measure of control over management practices.

These restrictive job definitions actually contributed to the alienating nature of factory work in the Fordist era. Yet once management had established this form of work organization as the norm, the unions were able to exercise power over management only by gaining control over job definitions, and by making sure these definitions were adhered to. The nature of union management relations was thus defined: the shop floor became the site of intricate rules and regulations which bound both management and labor to rigid job rules, task classifications, and seniority rights. As any slight violation of job rules by management could lead to a strike, an elaborate grievance system was established through which disagreements could be resolved. As a result of these dynamics, "the logic of the system of job classifications and seniority rights, and the judicial process by which they are supervised, operates to ensnare ever more of factory life in a net of rules with an ever finer mesh."[23]

3. CONCLUSION

This outline of the nature of the typical Fordist economy of the postwar years clarifies how both the macro- and micro-levels of the Fordist economic order functioned and how one depended upon and supported the other. This mass-production economy demanded a specific type of shop-floor organization, just as this specific type of shop-floor organization was economically successful only within the context of a mass-production/mass-consumption economy. By the early 1970s, however, the Fordist macro economy was beginning to show signs of crisis, and thus the system of shop-floor organization which underpinned this economy increasingly was called into question.

NOTES

1. Charles F. Sabel, *Work and Politics: The division of labor in industry* (New York: Cambridge University Press, 1982), p. 33.

2. Peter Gourevitch, *Politics in Hard Times: Comparative Responses to International Economic Crises* (Ithaca: Cornell University Press, 1986), p. 167.

3. Gourevitch (1986), p. 168. The importance of this last element will be borne out below.

4. Robert Boyer, "New Directions in Management Practices and Work Organization: General Principles and National Trajectories," CEPREMAP, CNRS, EHESS (Paris, August, 1991), p. 1.

5. Michael Piore and Charles Sabel, *The Second Industrial Divide: Possibilities for Prosperity* (New York: Basic Books, 1984), p. 79.

6. Andrew Glyn, Alan Hughes, Alain Lipietz, and Ajit Singh, "The Rise and Fall of the Golden Age," in Marglin and Schor, eds., *The Golden Age of Capitalism*, (Oxford: Clarendon Press, 1990), p. 43. Table 2.2.

7. This is not, however, to deny the increasing importance of international trade. While Fordist demand was primarily domestic, the search for demand led also to the development mechanisms designed to ensure open markets and free trade. This will be discussed in more detail below.

8. Glyn et al, p. 50.

9. Piore and Sabel, pp. 80 and 79. Also Glyn et al., pp. 57-58.

10. See Rianne Mahon, "From Fordism To ?: New Technology, Labour Markets and Unions," *Economic and Industrial Democracy*, Vol. 8, 1987.

11. Piore and Sabel, p. 84.

12. Piore and Sabel, p. 73.

13. Japan is a notable exception here. See Glyn et al., pp. 61-62; and footnote 10, p. 122.

14. Glyn et al., pp. 59-60.

15. Glyn et al., p. 62.

16. Gourevitch (1986), p. 167.

17. Nicholas Costello, Jonathan Michie, and Milne, *Beyond the Casino Economy: Planning for the 1990s* (New York: Verso Press, 1989), p. 20.

18. Glyn et al., p. 65.

19. Nonetheless, it is important to recall that Fordist growth was fueled primarily by domestic demand. The importance of the GATT may have been, as we shall see, less its effect on trade levels during the Fordist era, and more its effect of restricting member nation's ability to close off their markets in times of crisis, and to limit international exchange. Piore and Sabel, pp. 110-111.

20. This meant that Fordist factories ended up manufacturing huge quantities of the exact same product. The proto-typical example of this was the early Ford plant which produced only the Model-T Ford. Sabel, 1982, p. 33.

21. Glyn et al., pp. 55-56.

22. Raphael Kaplinsky, "Restructuring the capitalist labour process: some lessons from the car industry," *Cambridge Journal of Economics*. 12 (4) (December, 1988), p. 454.

23. Piore and Sabel, p. 114.

Chapter Two
The Crisis of Fordism

The Fordist era was, in the words of Marglin and Schor, the "Golden Age of Capitalism." During the period 1950-1973, GDP per capita in the advanced capitalist economies grew almost twice as fast as in any period since 1820, reaching an average rate of 3.8% growth, while total GDP grew at an average of 4.9% over the same period. Labor productivity during these years also grew "twice as fast as ever before," and there was a huge acceleration in the growth of the capital stock. Production and employment levels also increased dramatically throughout the period.[1] As described in Chapter One, these conditions promoted growth, both on the level of the macro-political economy and on the micro-level of the shop floor.

However, despite the fact that the economies of the advanced capitalist nations grew so quickly during these years, by the late 1960s the system was beginning to unravel, and by 1973 Fordism was visibly in crisis. The high rates of GDP growth, capital stock growth, and labor productivity, as well as the low inflation and low unemployment levels of the golden years, all began to give way. Expansion and boom were soon replaced by deep recession. The causes for the collapse of the system that had, for 25 years, been functioning (at least in economic terms) so well included both exogenous and endogenous factors. While exogenous factors certainly contributed to the crisis of the Fordist model, it was the endogenous causes which best explain why the economic order collapsed.

1. CAUSES OF THE CRISIS

Productivity Slowdown, Rising Wages, and Social Unrest

A first element in the crisis of the Fordist model of economic growth came with the slowdown, or "exhaustion," of the productivity

gains associated with the Fordist organization of work and the implementation of Fordist technology.[2] In the period 1973-1982, the average annual rate of increase of labor productivity (output per hour) dropped significantly when compared to the rates from 1960 to 1973. In the U.S., labor productivity growth dropped from 3% to 1.7%; in Germany from 5.7% to 3.6%; in France from 6.7% to 4.5%; in Great Britain from 4.4% to 1.8%; in Sweden from 6.6% to 2.7%; and in Japan from 10.7% to 7.2%.[3] This slowdown in productivity had severe implications for the Fordist model. Recall that the virtuous circle of Fordist growth was based on the tandem growth of productivity and wages. In this model, wage increases were based on increases in productivity levels, and as wages grew, demand expanded, and thus profits increased. Therefore, there was no conflict between wages and profits. In fact, wage growth was a prerequisite of economic growth and profit margins. With the slowdown in productivity growth, however, sustained wage growth meant decreasing profit margins — as wages outpaced productivity, increased wage costs were not compensated for by equally increasing levels of productivity and could thereby cut into profits. There subsequently developed an explicit conflict between wages and profits. This conflict represented a first crack in the virtuous circle of growth, and thus in the Fordist model itself.

This conflict between wages and profits arose, importantly, at a time when organized labor was in a position to secure its wage demands. This was the case for several reasons. The excess labor supplies available during the early postwar years had been depleted and thus no longer served as a buffer against wage demands. Further, without going into detail on this, as industry was populated increasingly by second-generation workers and decreasingly by first-generation workers, demands for wages (and improved working conditions) increased. In part due to the macro-economic policies, especially policies of full-employment, pursued during the Fordist years, labor markets had become tight. Largely as a result of these factors, unions had become very strong by the late 1960s. Indeed, as discussed in Chapter One, the Fordist model depended upon strong unions to formulate pattern wage bargaining. Thus while productivity levels were falling, the mechanisms that granted labor the power to demand higher wages remained in place. At least for a period, the conflict between wages and profits did not arrest the steady increase in wage levels. As wage increases continued to outpace productivity gains, two trends resulted.

The first was a spurt in inflation. As discussed in Chapter One, when wages grow faster than productivity, inflation is often the result.

As wages were indexed to prices, a spiral of inflation indeed resulted. Between 1967 and 1971 inflation rose in the U.S. from 2.8% to 4.3%; in Germany, from 4.0% to 6.1%; in France, from 2.7% to 5.5%; in Great Britain, from 2.5% to 9.4%; in Sweden, from 4.3% to 7.4%; and in Japan, from 4.0% to 6.1%.[4] Inflation, of course, is anathema to the Fordist model of growth. Mass production investments require stability and call for predictable markets in order to enable investors to make long-range investment decisions. Yet with inflation, this market stability and predictability is lost. Inflation, as caused by the outpacing of productivity gains by wage gains, cut deeply into the Fordist model.

Inflation, however, was not the only deleterious effect of the rising wages of the late 1960s and early 1970s. By 1973 the share of profits in net value added had declined by almost 25% in the U.S., Japan, and Europe as compared with the peak shares secured during the 1950s and 1960s. This declining profit share was a direct result of the rising share of wages in net value added, itself the result of declining rates of productivity growth. Recall, however, that another segment of the "virtuous circle" was the transformation of high profit rates into high rates of investment. As wages claimed a higher share of value added and profit rates fell, there was less capital available for investment. This drop in investment levels represented another crack in the virtuous circle of Fordist growth. In summation of these trends, Glyn et al. write:

> If productivity growth falters because of problems in the system of production, and is not sufficiently matched by a corresponding moderation of real wage growth . . . then pressures on profit margins and capital ratios may threaten the macroeconomic structure.[5]

Declining productivity levels and sustained wage growth also had an impact on government policy. Governments in the Fordist era had been committed to stabilizing both domestic and international markets in order to assure steady and adequate demand for mass-production industry. In the international arena, the primary role of the state had been stabilizing trade through securing exchange rate parity. Exchange parity is not threatened by wage growth as long as productivity gains keep pace with this growth. However, when wage gains exceed productivity growth and inflation sets in, exchange rate parity is indeed threatened. The inflation of the late 1960s and early 1970s therefore forced governments concerned with maintaining fixed international parity to either deflate their economies or place controls on wages.

Calls for voluntary wage restraint were made, and in some cases statutory controls were imposed. Both options marked a clear break from the policies of the past decades, where steady expansion of wages was a primary goal.[6]

As the government became increasingly involved in the economy and increasingly concerned with controlling wage growth there was a tendency towards heightened centralization of collective bargaining. The more centralized wage negotiations became, the easier it was for governments to influence their outcomes. A motivating factor in the formation of these corporatist bargaining structures, as shown in Chapter One, was the control they provided unions over wage demands. Increasingly in the late 1960s and early 1970s, governments demanded that unions exercise their control over wage demands and institute wage restraint. This development marked a threat to grass-roots, or firm level, autonomy in organized labor. The conjunction of these wage restrictions—which contributed to the loss of local autonomy in the labor movement—and very low rates of unemployment led to a period of fairly extreme social unrest across the advanced capitalist countries in the late 1960s. As Glyn et al. put it:

> In the tightening European labor market in the late 1960s the response to interrupted real wage growth, and the erosion of locally based negotiating procedures and work practices was a wave of predominantly unofficial, plant-led strikes.[7]

It is important to note four ways in which this new labor militancy was an element of the crisis of Fordism. The most explicit attack on Fordism came as a direct assault by workers on the Fordist methods of production. According to Boyer, automobile workers in the 1960s rebelled against the "boring character of assembly line tasks," and challenged the Fordist methods themselves.[8] In his book *Alternatives to Lean Production*, Christian Berggren also argues that the strikes of the 1960s stemmed from workers objection to Fordism. According to Berggren, autoworkers objected to the fact that they could not vary the pace of their own work, to the repetitive nature of their work, to the difficulty in "gain[ing] a sense of purpose by orienting their efforts to the completion of a task," and to the intense time pressures imposed by the Fordist organization.[9] These objections indicated that the "compromise" of the Fordist years, i.e. good and rising wages in exchange for boring and repetitive work, was no longer acceptable to

many production workers. The facts of union strength and tight labor markets lent these objections significant strength.

In addition, the social unrest of the late 1960s represented a component of the crisis of Fordism in several other ways. First, the labor militancy was associated with increased wage pressures, and increased pressures for wage indexation. These demands pushed wage growth ahead of productivity gains, leading to destabilizing inflation. Second, labor peace had been secured, to a large extent, throughout the Fordist years as part of the Fordist "compromise," which guaranteed the stability necessary to facilitate mass production. The strike waves marked an end to this labor peace, and thus represented another blow to the stability of the Fordist era. Third, and finally, the Fordist era was one in which large and, to varying degrees, centralized unions symbolized a united voice for production workers. Indeed, these centralized unions were necessary components of the wage bargaining structures that were such an important part of the Fordist growth dynamic. However, the unofficial wildcat strikes of the 1960s indicated that workers had lost confidence in these large, centralized Fordist unions. Another element of the Fordist model, another contributor to Fordist stability, had thus come under attack.

Productivity slowdown, continuing wage increases and the social unrest of the late 1960s and the early 1970s had broken the virtuous circle of Fordist growth. Wages and productivity could no longer expand together the way they had in the 1950s and 1960s, and investment was similarly discouraged. Inflation and labor unrest meant the beginning of the end of stable markets both domestically and internationally, and thus the end of the Fordist model itself.

Inflation, Deficits, and Flexible Exchange Rates

International stability, as secured by the Bretton Woods agreements, which established a fixed exchange rate system underpinned by the U.S. dollar and Fort Knox gold, was another victim of the crisis years of the late 1960s and early 1970s. The successful functioning of this system was dependent upon two things: the ability and willingness of member countries to tailor domestic policies in order to maintain exchange rate parity and the willingness of member countries to hold their reserves in dollars and to settle international accounts with dollar payments. The system was facilitated throughout the postwar years by a strong dollar—itself the product of a strong U.S. economy with low inflation and no deficits. In the late 1960s, however, the components that had held this system together began to deteriorate.

First, U.S. unwillingness to fund the Vietnam War through higher taxes led to increased inflation and deficit spending. These developments, in conjunction with the United States' declining position in world trading markets, undermined the strength of the dollar and led to international speculation against the currency. This speculation further weakened the dollar and European countries became less willing to hold U.S. dollars as their currency of international exchange and reserve. In order to stop this run on the dollar, the U.S. would have had to abandon its inflationary and deficit spending policies, and thus fashion its domestic policies to the needs of the international order. The U.S. was not willing to do this, and therefore abandoned the gold standard, and thereby the Bretton Woods exchange rate system.

Although developments in the United States certainly undermined the Fordist international economy, developments in Europe also contributed to its demise. Europe at this time was dealing with inflationary and wage pressures of its own. The labor militancy of the 1960s put pressure on governments to maintain wages and to increase wage and price indexations, which caused inflation. Further, the recession into which all advanced capitalist countries were slipping meant that a smaller and smaller tax base had to support an expanding social welfare bill. This was the case especially because the social welfare programs of the Fordist years were designed to "automatically stabilize" markets by increasing payouts during slumps in the business cycle. In order to maintain these social welfare programs, larger and larger government deficits were required. The ability to allow inflationary wage growth, and the freedom to engage in deficit spending was thus necessary for European governments, especially in the face of labor militancy. Like the U.S., therefore, European nations were no longer willing to tailor their domestic policies in order to maintain exchange rate parity. Thus, in place of the fixed exchange rate system, a floating exchange rate regime was established, in which currency values would float relative to other currencies, in order to allow inflation and deficit spending.

The floating exchange rate system was designed to insulate domestic economies from the policies of other nations. However, the price of the new system was international economic instability. Having replaced the stabilized international economy based on a strong U.S. dollar, the floating exchange rate system thus became another destabilizing element of the crisis of Fordism. This was due primarily to changes in the nature of international currency markets: in a flexible exchange rate system, though not in a fixed exchange rate system, a shift in demand for a country's currency changes the price of tradable

products. If demand for the Swedish krona goes up, the price of Swedish goods on the international market will go up as well. Demand for currency, moreover, is dependent on non-economic factors, such as political stability, so that under floating rates it becomes nearly impossible to predict the value of a currency, especially over long time periods. As a result of these currency fluctuations, it becomes nearly impossible to predict international prices over long time periods. As Piore and Sabel put it:

> The shift to floating exchange rates made the price of goods in international trade hostage to forces only distantly connected to national economic performance—and almost impossible to forecast and control.[10]

This became a significant problem as a result of the growth of currency flows and currency speculation, which greatly outpaced the level of actual foreign trade in the 1970s. Thus the stability required by mass-production investment decisions and provided by the Fordist international economic order was lost in the shift to floating exchange rates.

Market Saturation and the Growth of International Trade

Another component of Fordism's collapse was the saturation of markets for industrial products. Throughout the Fordist years, productive capacity was increasing rapidly and was balanced by rapid increases in demand. However, after almost 30 years of the production of the same products, consumer markets were becoming saturated. For example, in the early 1950s only 25% of Americans had cars and only 47% of American households had televisions. The challenge for these industries in the 1950s, then, was to produce these consumer durables as quickly as possible and to be sure that consumers had the buying power necessary to purchase the mass produced goods. Yet by the 1970s, one in two Americans had a car and 99% of American households had a television set. Likewise, greater than 90% of American households had clothes washers, toasters, and vacuum cleaners, and more than 99% had refrigerators, radios, and irons.[11]

As a result, the industrial strategy of mass production for mass markets ran into trouble. No longer could expansion be based on matching increasing productivity with increasing domestic demand. The original response to this economic development was the attempt on the

part of the advanced capitalist countries to penetrate other advanced capitalist domestic markets. A marked expansion of foreign trade did indeed take place in the early 1970s, and the trade that took place involved the consumer durables for which domestic economies had become saturated. In the "developed market economies," total exports in current dollars rose from 10% of GDP in 1960-1970, to 25.2% in 1970-1974.[12] While trade clearly increased, this strategy of international market expansion was unable to resolve the dilemma of market saturation which continued to undermine the logic of an economy based on domestic consumption.[13]

More importantly for our purposes here, as trade increased, a greater and greater proportion of demand came from overseas, and the domestic market was correspondingly of decreasing importance to the Fordist firms. The decreasing importance of the domestic market led firms, and states, to understand wages less as a source of demand and increasingly as a cost. This, of course, worked to undercut the basis of the Fordist compromise. The institutions designed to balance demand and productivity, the core of macro-Fordism, only made sense in a context where *domestic* demand constituted the primary source of mass demand. Moreover high and rising wages were exchanged for labor acceptance of boring, repetitive work and labor peace. With the growth of trade, the logic of the Fordist compromise, at both the macro- and micro-levels, was undermined.

Supply Shocks, Changes in Domestic Policy, and Recession: The End of Fordism

These elements of the crisis arose mainly as a result of the workings of Fordism itself, but there were two significant exogenous variables which contributed to Fordism's collapse. The first of these, as reported by Piore and Sabel, was the Russian wheat deal. After a series of bad harvests in the Soviet Union, the Soviets were forced to use United States wheat surpluses to survive the shortages. The U.S. had kept these surpluses of wheat stocks as a buffer to stabilize world agricultural prices, a policy clearly in line with the many other stabilization policies employed by the advanced capitalist countries in the Fordist years. However, the agreement to sell wheat to the Soviets completely exhausted this buffer stock. The result was that, for the first time in the postwar period, agricultural prices became volatile. The initial impact of the wheat deal was a rise in food prices due to an effective food shortage. Food prices, as was the case with any commodity, were indexed to wages, and as such a rise in the price of

food meant the beginning of another inflationary spiral. This inflation, of course, plagued the stability required by mass-production industry. More important, however, was the loss of stability suffered as a result of the increasing volatility of prices occasioned by the loss of the wheat buffer.[14]

Similar, though more severe developments followed the oil shocks of 1973 and 1979. Stability in oil prices had been secured throughout the postwar era as a result of flexible oil production. That is, shifts in demand led to higher or lower production rather than to higher or lower prices. With the Arab oil embargo and OPEC, however, oil-producing nations decided collectively to curtail the production of oil. This meant that oil prices, like food prices, were to become volatile; changes in demand would lead to changes in price, rather than changes in production levels. Again, the initial impact of the oil shock was a rise in prices, which led to more inflation. The inflation was quite damaging, but again the loss of stability occasioned by the new volatility in energy costs was more significant in the long run. As Piore and Sabel write, "This was exactly the kind of uncertainty that mass producers—with their long-term investment in high-fixed-cost, specialized assets—found most difficult to manage. Should they plan production on the assumption of low energy prices or high ones?"[15] On two more fronts, then, the stability so important to and secured by the Fordist model faced attack.

Perhaps the most significant effect of the supply shocks, however, was their impact on domestic economic policy. For national governments, the supply shocks represented yet another boost to already high and increasing levels of inflation. States in the postwar era had been consistently concerned with securing adequate and stable levels of demand to support mass-production industry. These policies had been maintained into the early 1970s, but they began to change. The supply shocks induced national governments to shift their domestic economic policy from one of expansion to one of restraint. Unemployment, in the Fordist era a threat to collective consumption power, was used increasingly as a tool to fight inflation. And interest rates, kept low during the Fordist years to ensure extensive investment, were pushed up to dampen the inflationary spiral. As a result of these restrictive policies, the advanced capitalist economies were driven into recession.

The onset of this prolonged recession indicated to many that government involvement in the economy, which had been relatively extensive in the Fordist era, did more to hinder economic growth than it did to promote growth. As a result, another shift in public policy occurred: states moved away from Keynesianism and toward

deregulation and a restoration of market logic and pressure. While the degree to which these changes were implemented varied across countries, there was a general trend away from the stabilizing role that governments had played throughout the Fordist years. These changes deepened the destabilization of the crisis years. As Piore and Sabel write:

> These efforts at governmental 'deregulation' were an attack on the institutions that had created and maintained the stability presupposed by mass production . . . Their effect, in the short run, was to exacerbate the confusion introduced by the economic crisis.[16]

With the recession of the early 1970s, the end of the Fordist era was evident. The "virtuous circle" had been reversed: as a result of the recession there was a marked decline in demand, which led to a drop in profits, which led to a drop in investments and an increase in unemployment, which further dampened demand, and so on. The entire Fordist era had been built on growth: as the economy grew, wages and investments increased, and thus more growth was secured. The Fordist "compromise" was an exchange of high wages and an extensive welfare state for labor's acceptance of boring jobs and the basic capitalist economy. With the recession, however, this type of exchange was no longer quite so possible. As Gourevitch puts it, "With the breakdown of growth, the possibility of meeting the terms for . . . the 'postwar settlements' was called into question."[17] In this respect, then, the recession marked the end of the Fordist era.

The recession marked the end of Fordism in another fundamental way. Above all else, the Fordist model was built to solve the crisis of demand posed so clearly by the Great Depression and to ensure the economic conditions required by mass-production industry. Meeting these goals implied providing adequate consumption levels for the mass-production economy and providing the stability necessitated by the long production runs and high-cost capital investments of mass-production industry. As a result of all of the critical developments outlined in this chapter, in conjunction with the restrictive government policies these developments engendered, however, the recession of the 1970s turned out to be yet another crisis of demand. Without adequate demand, the consumption levels and the stability required by mass-production industry began to slip away once again. The recession which resulted from the cumulative impacts of the crisis of Fordism led to, as

Piore and Sabel put it, "Confusion [which] led to the breakup of mass markets for standardized products. It did so by reducing the portion of demand that employers saw as sufficiently long-term to justify the long-term fixed-cost investments of mass production."[18] With the postwar settlements threatened, and demand once again declining and destabilized, the Fordist economic regime had crumbled.

2. IMPLICATIONS OF THE CRISIS

From Instability to Flexibility

In Sabel's words, "Anything that unsettles prospects of manufacturing a certain product in a fixed way and selling it in predictably large numbers for a foreseeable price undermines the propensity to invest in the Fordist strategy."[19] This chapter has outlined a whole series of developments which acted to undermine the stability of the Fordist era. As Sabel points out, with the loss of market stability that was necessary for the survival of the Fordist model, the logic that lay behind the Fordist way of running the economy no longer seemed so convincing. The crisis of Fordism posed challenges to the Fordist economic order and provided impetus for change on both the micro- and macro-levels.

With the breakdown of stabilized mass markets, as outlined above, the Fordist model of shop-floor organization was no longer quite as attractive to industrialists.[20] And, with the disintegration of these stable mass markets, the production goals of industry needed to change. Although managers, in the main, were not making these realizations in the early 1970s, it was the developments of these years which would eventually force significant adaptation. Primarily, with the loss of mass markets, manufacture of mass quantities of standardized goods no longer made so much sense. No longer could a firm expect to profit by producing more and more of the same car, refrigerator, television set, etc. There was, therefore, a need for product innovation.[21] The importance of this forced shift in product strategy lies in the fact that the demand for new, diversified products called for a new organization of work.

If the Fordist era was defined by stability, the era which began with the crisis of Fordism was primarily an era of instability. While stabilized mass markets supported mass production of standardized goods, the economic context following the crisis of Fordism called for a

more flexible manufacturing style. With volatile demand levels, domestic price levels, and international currency prices, it was necessary for industry to adapt quickly to reconfigurations of the market. Additionally, as markets for mass-produced goods became saturated, the constitution of demand became more specialized. As a result, firms began focusing on "niche" markets and on the ability to continually shift from one niche to another. On the shop floor, this meant embracing, to some degree, a more flexible organization of production, and employing less specialized and more flexible machinery. Thus, while the crisis of Fordism implied the end of the Fordist organization of work on the shop floor, it also implied the potential for positive change. Beyond the production of new, specialized products, the crisis also facilitated a move away from the Fordist organization of work.

The new economic context, however, while delimiting the form that the new organization of production would take, does not determine its form.[22] The form that work reorganization took in each country would depend upon the interaction of these economic conditions with the balance of power between different societal actors and the access each of these actors has to decision making mechanisms. Among the most important of these actors are, of course, organized labor, business, and the state. Moreover, the form of work reorganization that each national economy develops will have critical implications for the lives of those who labor under the dictates of the new production paradigms.

Union-Management Relations

While the changes in shop-floor organization are perhaps the most essential development resulting from the crisis of Fordism, Fordism's crisis has had important implications for union-management relations as well. First, as discussed in Chapter One, a primary role for Fordist unions was securing wage agreements through collective bargaining with management and, in some cases, with the state. The wage agreements were a primary component of demand stabilization. Yet, as discussed earlier, wage gains in the late 1960s and early 1970s began to outpace productivity gains, and thus became inflationary. Moreover, as the importance of trade increased, domestic wages increasingly constituted a cost for the firm and decreasingly constituted demand. Therefore, with the crisis of Fordism, the unions' role in securing continuous wage increases was challenged. The changing economic context had made this role less tenable, at least in the eyes of business concerned with maintaining internationally competitive prices.

As Turner writes in *Democracy at Work,* as a result of these "market driven imperatives," union emphasis on wage gains has declined and has been replaced by a focus on issues of work reorganization—"conflicts and negotiations that precede or accompany managerial attempts to reorganize work."[23] Of course, this change in union strategy is not only a result of the decreasing tenability of continuing wage increases, but is also a response to worker demands and the new interest, on the part of management, in reorganizing work. While the situation is different in each country, across all nations unions' ability to influence the nature of work reorganizations is dependent on union strength—determined, in large part, by organizational density, the level at which organization takes place (i.e., firm, industry, nation), and the unions' ability to formulate their own agenda independent of managerial influence—as well as the presence or absence of corporatist bargaining structures and/or protective labor laws.[24]

Another implication of the crisis for union-management relations is the trend toward decentralization of bargaining. As a result of the shift in focus toward issues of work organization, and because work reorganization takes place at the plant level, plant-level bargaining has become increasingly important. The impact that this decentralization has on unions in each country is again dependent on union strength, influence in managerial decision-making structures, and the presence and/or absence of corporatist bargaining structures, etc. Second, the Fordist model of production called for a specific form of union-management relations on the shop floor. Specifically, unions were mainly concerned with enforcing strict job definitions. As the organization of the shop floor changed, to keep up with changes in the broader economic context, this form of shop-floor relations was challenged: the "web" of regulations that arose in the Fordist era is hardly consummate with flexible production. Thus the form that post-Fordist production takes in each country will not only shape the organization of the shop floor, but will delimit the form of shop-floor relations between unions and management. Again, the power and access to decision-making mechanisms that unions and business have will be crucial in determining the form that these relations take within the context of flexible production systems.

3. CONCLUSION

Following several decades of economic success, the Fordist model had fallen into collapse, and within the context of Fordism's crisis, the search for non-Fordist production models and non-Fordist systems of work organization became imperative. The mass-production work systems which had afforded competitive success in the Fordist economic system were no longer satisfactory. In order to compete in these destabilized post-Fordist markets, firms had to develop non-Fordist work systems which allowed, above all else, flexible production. The following two chapters explore the development of two models of such flexible, non-Fordist work systems. By understanding how these systems evolved, it will be possible to understand the conditions which shaped the ways in which these work systems achieved productive flexibility. In both the Japanese and Swedish cases, economic conditions which demanded productive flexibility interacted with the relative power of business and labor to produce very different reorganizations of work.

NOTES

1. Glyn et al, "The Rise and Fall of the Golden Age," in Marglin and Schor, Op cit., pp. 41, 42, and 49.

2. Paul Hirst and Jonathan Zeitlin, "Flexible Specialization vs Post-Fordism: Theory, Evidence, and Policy Implications," Birkbeck Policy Centre Working Paper (Bloomsbury, London, May 1990), p. 18.

3. Pierre Tabatoni, "The Market Economies Tack Against the Wind: Coping with Economic Shocks 1973-1983," in Industrial Relations Research Association Series, *Industrial Relations in a Decade of Economic Change* (Illinois: Pantagraph Printing, 1985), p. 5. Glyn et al., in fact, date the beginnings of the productivity slowdown to several years before 1973.

4. Tabatoni, p. 7. There were other causes for this inflation, as I will discuss below.

5. Glyn et al., p. 73.

6. Glyn et al., p. 93; and footnote 26, p. 93.

7. Glyn et al., p. 93. The excerpt continues, "Only Japan with less severe labour market pressure escaped relatively unscathed." In chapter four I will discuss the wave of wildcat strikes that hit Sweden in 1969-70.

8. Boyer, "New Directions in Management Practices and Work Organization," Op cit., p. 3.

9. Christian Berggren, *Alternatives to Lean Production: Work Organization in the Swedish Auto Industry* (Ithaca: ILR Press, 1992), pp. 4-5.

10. Piore and Sabel, *The Second Industrial Divide*, Op cit., pp. 173-174.

11. Piore and Sabel, p. 184.

12. Glyn et al., p. 111, table 2.22.

13. The failure of extension into international markets in solving the dilemma of market saturation eventually gave rise to a strategy of product differentiation. That is, if standardized products no longer sold, firms began seeing the necessity for varying the products they produced. This of course marks a significant departure from the Fordist model.

14. Piore and Sabel, pp. 175-176.

15. Piore and Sabel, p. 176.

16. Piore and Sabel, pp. 181-182.

17. Peter Gourevitch, Andrew Martin, George Ross, Christopher Allen, Stephen Bornstein; Andrei Markovits, *Unions and Economic Crisis: Britain, West Germany and Sweden* (Boston: George Allen and Unwin), p. 2.

18. Piore and Sabel, p. 183.

19. Sabel (1982), p. 195.

20. Sabel (1982), p. 194.

21. These developments were applicable in varying degrees in different industries. As relates to the topic of this book, they quite definitely applied to the automobile industry.

22. Throughout the literature on this period, scholars develop very different versions of what the post-Fordist production paradigm may or may not eventually look like. For example, in *Work and Politics*, Sabel offers two possibilities, "Neo-Fordism" and the "High Technology Cottage Industry." (Sabel (1982), pp. 209-227) In his book *Postindustrial Possibilities*, Fred Block argues that the post-Fordist economy may or may not be organized around what he terms "qualitative growth." (Fred Block, *Postindustrial Possibilities: A Critique of Economic Discourse* (Berkeley: University of California Press, 1990), pp. 189-190.) Piore and Sabel, of course, offer their

vision of "flexible specialization." Finally, management periodicals and texts from the past decade are full of glowing reviews of the "Japanese model" of production organization; argue that this model will define the post-Fordist economy.

23. Lowell Turner, *Democracy at Work* (Ithaca: Cornell University Press, 1991), p. 2.

24. Turner, p. 2.

Chapter Three
The Preconditions for Work Changes in the Japanese Automobile Industry

Following the oil shock of 1973, and with the general crisis of the Fordist economic order, advanced capitalist economies began to suffer a prolonged recession. Something had clearly gone wrong. The institutions and economic strategies that had solved the problems of the postwar years were not able to sustain economic success in the changed world economy. While these Western economies struggled through the early years of the crisis watching their leading industrial firms suffer with lower productivity levels and declining profit margins, however, the Japanese automobile industry was coming through the crisis years relatively unscathed. As the Big Three in the U.S. and European automakers tried to keep afloat amid declining demand and saturated markets, Toyota was able to maintain its pre-crisis profit levels.[1] As a result of the success of Japanese automakers in coping with the crisis of Fordism and the world recession it brought, many began to look to Japan for a way to solve the economic test posed by the crisis. For many, the Japanese model of work organization thus came to represent a crucial component of economic success in the post-Fordist era.

Yet while the model of work organization employed at Toyota and Nissan in the 1970s may have represented the solution to the crisis of Fordism to Western observers, this system of work organization was not developed in response to that crisis. In fact, the model of work organization which became so popular in the 1970s and 1980s was developed in the 1950s. While the Western advanced capitalist countries were developing the institutions of the Fordist economic order, the Japanese were already developing a system of flexible production which, nearly three decades later, would come to be known as the model of post-Fordist production. In other words, while the Japanese model of work organization represented a flexible alternative to traditional Fordist production methods—and was therefore suitable to post-Fordist markets—it was not originally a post-Fordist system.

This chapter outlines the factors that led to the implementation of the work changes in the Japanese auto industry, and explains why this reorganization of work took the form it did. An understanding of the development of this system of work organization reveals two things: where Japan fits into the model of Fordism/crisis of Fordism and, more importantly, why the Japanese system developed the way it did—why productive flexibility was achieved in this particular way. Finally, understanding the evolution of this system will clarify the predicates of the system's success. This will prove especially useful in the comparative study of the Swedish model, discussed later.

1. FORDISM IN JAPAN?

An important component of this book is the portrayal of the relationship between the collapse of the Fordist economic order and the development of new forms of work organization. Therefore, the first question this chapter seeks to answer is whether the Japanese model of work organization evolved in response to the crisis of Fordism. A simple look at the chronological development of the major elements of the Japanese system shows that either Fordism developed and went into crisis earlier in Japan than in the Western nations, or that the Japanese model of work organization did not evolve in response to the crisis of Fordism. While the crisis began around 1973, the new Japanese work organization had basically evolved by the middle of the 1960s. For example, the Just-in-Time production process (explained below), so highly touted today as a major departure from the Fordist production strategy, was implemented at Toyota in the early 1950s. The Just-in-Time system was extended to supplier firms and used in delivery operations as early as the 1950s as well.[2] Simple kanbans (explained below), were first used in 1953, and were used throughout all of Toyota by 1965. Toyota started doing mixed assembly in the late 1950s, and was producing in small lot sizes in the 1950s as well. Finally, by the mid-1950s, Toyota workers were each operating, on average, five to ten machines, in contrast to the Fordist system where each worker was responsible for one machine only.[3]

Did Japan, then, go through a period of Fordism earlier than the Western advanced capitalist countries, and did the new model of work organization, in this way, evolve out of Fordism? It does not appear that this is the case. Recall that Fordism developed to address several critical problems experienced by advanced capitalism in the 1930s.

Primary among these problems was a crisis of underconsumption. In response to the crisis of underconsumption, business, labor, and the state developed institutions which cumulatively constituted the Fordist order. But, as Alice Amsden points out, the economic conditions present in late industrializing countries—of which Japan is one—are very different than the conditions which gave rise to Fordism. Underconsumption is not the main impediment to growth in a late industrializing country such as Japan. Rather, the main "problem" was one of "raising productivity and creating international competitiveness, not effective demand."[4]

Elements of the Japanese political economy of the late 1940s and early 1950s indicate that very few of the typically Fordist institutions or conditions were present. It will be helpful to identify some of these briefly. First, stable mass markets for standardized goods, a critical element of the Fordist economy, did not exist in early postwar Japan. Not only were markets small in Japan, especially relative to the mass markets of typical Fordist nations, but demand, at least in auto, was fairly differentiated; that is, standardized goods were never sought after in Japan as they were in Western advanced capitalist countries. As a result, the Japanese economy departed from the Fordist model in a second significant way: by the 1950s export markets were sought as a key to increasing demand (see below). As it was the centrality of domestic demand which implied a series of domestically focused demand stabilization devices and the development of a domestic welfare state, these institutions were hereby less functional, and less present, in Japan. Third, the defeat of the independent Japanese labor movement in the early 1950s deprived Japan of what in the Fordist nations was a central element in wage stabilization.

As such, it is inaccurate to assume that the Japanese economy went through a form of abbreviated Fordism and that subsequently the new Japanese model of work organization developed as a response to this. While the Japanese system of work organization may prove useful to Western capitalist nations in addressing the crisis of Fordism, this system evolved under a set of conditions unique to Japan. The remainder of this chapter examines the three central elements in the evolution of the Japanese system of work organization: the state, the labor movement, and the economic environment of the early postwar years.

2. THE PRECONDITIONS FOR CHANGE

The Impact of the State

While much political-economy writing on the Japanese state focuses on strong state-business relations, the role of MITI, etc., in the years following World War II, these were not the essential components of the government's role in the economy. By the 1950s strong ties between the state and business were reemerging, and MITI was beginning to play a role in the automobile sector, as discussed below. However, in the immediate postwar years the most significant state activity, especially as related to the evolution of the new system of work organization, was the American Occupation force's shifting economic policies and attitudes toward labor unions. As Andrew Gordon writes, "The reforms of the American Occupation defined a new legal and political framework within which the events of the first postwar decade unfolded."[5]

When the American Occupation began, the ideology which underlay SCAP's (the Supreme Commander for Allied Forces) economic policies was the drive to "democratize" Japan and curb the power of the *zaibatsus*, the large Japanese corporate conglomerates. Both goals could be addressed, SCAP believed, through the development of an independent labor movement. As such, SCAP implemented legal changes which supported the development of labor unions throughout Japanese industry. The Labor Union Law of 1945 guaranteed workers the right to organize, bargain collectively, and strike, and protected workers against discrimination for union activity. Two other laws, the Labor Relations Adjustment Law (1946) and the Labor Standards Law (1947) also encouraged and protected the development of a strong and independent labor union movement. Perhaps equally as important as these new labor laws was SCAP's ideological support for the development of an independent union movement.

Indeed, with SCAP's support for the union movement, workers in Japanese industries began to organize at unprecedented rates. Before the changes implemented by the American forces, effectively 0% of the Japanese work force was organized. By 1946, however, almost 5 million workers made up 17,000 labor unions.[6] By 1949, 56% of that work force had organized, and perhaps even more significantly, by 1953 18 of Japan's largest industries had organized labor federations. After enterprise-level unions had been formed at Nissan, Toyota, and Isuzu,

representatives from these unions met in 1947 and formed the All-Japan Automobile Industry Union (Zenji).[7] The enterprise unions may have remained the primary bargaining organization throughout Japan, but the 1940s saw a definite emergence of a drive for industrial unions.

The difference between the early postwar enterprise unions and the emerging industrial unions would become crucial in the years to come. After the war, workers began forming unions organized around their individual companies. While these unions were based on the individual firm, they were independent of management in the early postwar years. That is, in contrast to the enterprise unions formed in the early 1950s, these company-based unions were able to formulate their own demands and policy agendas for the operation of their firms, and often voiced militant demands. In their independence from management then, the enterprise unions formed in the immediate postwar years were stronger than the enterprise unions formed in the 1950s.[8]

Nonetheless, the power and autonomy of any union organized on the level of an individual firm is greatly restricted because the success of that union, and its workers, is tied to the success of the firm. Because of this, there was also a drive in the early postwar years to organize the company-based unions into broader industrial and national confederations, which are able to exercise greater autonomy and power vis-a-vis employers since they are not dependent on the success of individual firms. The failure of the movement to organize and sustain an industrial labor confederation, and the emergence of ineffectual, managerially dominated enterprise unions was intimately connected with the development of work changes in the Japanese auto industry.

SCAP policy toward the unions led, moreover, not only to the enormous blossoming of union organizing on both the company and confederative levels, but to union radicalism as well. As Halberstam explains, "Japan had almost no history of moderate trade unionism,"[9] and when unions began to develop after the war their leadership came almost entirely from the Communists. As economic conditions worsened, union radicalism grew more rampant. In 1946, 157,000 workers were involved with the "production-control movement," during which several factories were seized, management was thrown out, and production was carried on by the work force without management aid or intervention.[10]

Perhaps the most significant display of union radicalism, however, was the general strike called for February 1, 1947. Before the strike date, SCAP was predicting that close to 6 million workers would participate.[11] Clearly then, the Japanese labor movement had gone from a state of virtual nonexistence to a highly organized and radicalized

movement in the course of several years. The influence of SCAP policy toward the labor movement is also clear.

The general economic policy originally imposed by SCAP also aided in the development and radicalization of the Japanese labor movement. SCAP's original economic policy objective was to increase industrial production and, to this end, state subsidies were granted to manufacturers, and inflation control was not targeted as a policy priority. Such policy commitments to economic expansion provided a context in which union demands (i.e., for wage increases) were feasible, and indeed the unions met with significant success in securing their demands. Moreover, as Gordon points out, this union success did not dampen radicalism but rather "led to more union growth and militance."[12] As union demands were met, partly as a result of expansionist economic policies, workers were encouraged to voice more demands and to continue organizing.

It was not for long, however, that an American occupying force would remain supportive of so radical a union movement. The change in SCAP's approach to the new unions, and the change in its general economic policy, began to develop in the late 1940s as a result of a dramatic shift in U.S. foreign policy. When the U.S. accepted that China was to become a communist nation under Mao, Japan became crucial to the United States' Cold War policy: Japan was to be the American roadblock to communism in Asia.[13] With this shift in the role that the U.S. intended for Japan came a shift in the general ideology that underlay SCAP policy. Rather than concerning itself with the weakening of the Japanese *zaibatsu* and with economic democracy, SCAP now focused its energies on building a "strong Japan." This policy shift implied strengthening Japanese industry and, therefore, did not bode well for the new Japanese labor movement.

The most obvious manifestation of this changing American approach to Japan came with the SCAP clamp down on union activity. Although SCAP had been critical of the most extreme forms of union radicalism as early as 1946, in 1948 and 1949 legal changes were implemented which were designed to restrict the "political" activity of unions. The Labor Union Law was revised to weaken private sector unions and to prohibit public sector unions from striking.[14] In addition to these legal changes SCAP, under MacArthur's orders, banned the general strike which had been called for February 1947. The banning of the strike clearly displayed the new hostility of the American forces to the burgeoning labor movement and had two critical effects on the future development of the Japanese labor movement. First, it prevented a nationwide display of working-class protest and, as such, represented a

major setback to the development of a national Japanese union. The planned unification of Sanbetsu (the Congress of Industrial Unions) and Sodomei (the Japan Federation of Labor) into a national labor federation was obstructed by SCAP's action, greatly affecting the nature of unionism in Japan. As Moore writes, "By preventing the unification of the unions, the SCAP doomed as well the fight to make industrial unions the basic means for worker organization in Japan."[15]

The second major effect of the SCAP strike ban was the message sent to businesses and labor groups. While SCAP had firmly backed unions and union development in the immediate postwar years, its allegiance had now shifted. The renunciation of this support and the new backing given to Japanese business was crucial to the reemergence of business strength, just as the support given to unions by SCAP in these early years was crucial to the developing strength of the labor movement. Significantly, in the same year that the general strike was banned and the Sanbetsu/Sodomei merger obstructed, SCAP allowed the formation of a national employers federation, Nikkeiren, which it had forbidden as recently as 1946. Upon its formation, Nikkeiren immediately began launching attacks at what it deemed the "excessive" power of labor.[16]

Then, in 1949 and 1950, SCAP, in conjunction with the Japanese government and with the support of Nikkeiren, took its most severe step against union radicalism by supporting a Red Purge. During the purge, approximately 12,000 workers who had been deemed "Communist Party members or sympathizers" were fired and prohibited from participating in the unions. Concurrent with the Red Purge, the Americans began to encourage the development of "democratic cells" within the unions, which further de-radicalized the unions.[17] The general impact of these measures was clear: the increasing strength of labor was checked, and managerial authority was enhanced. As Gordon puts it, "These steps to thwart radical, political union activities, and limit the rights of both public and private sector workers, helped bring about the revival of management authority."[18]

SCAP's changed policies toward unions, however, were not the only factor in the reassertion of managerial strength. In February 1949 Joseph Dodge, a new American economic emissary, was sent to Japan to end inflation and curb government deficits. Just as expansionist economic policies during the immediate postwar years were important in fostering the success of union demands, the implementation of this "Dodge line," a clear reversal of earlier economic policy, was critical in weakening the unions. It was through Dodge's economic policy that a strong, capitalist Japan was to be developed. Although Japan did

eventually recover from the postwar period, the Dodge line initially deepened the severity of the Japanese postwar recession. The Dodge line cut demand, reduced incomes, and led to even higher levels of unemployment. Further, in the attempt to cut government deficits, government subsidies to business, used previously to aid in the expansion of production, were cut.

The effects on workers and the labor movement were harsh. Hundreds of thousands of workers became unemployed under the Dodge Line as thousands of small and medium-sized companies were forced into bankruptcy. In addition, management used the cuts in subsidies and the need to cut wages and employment levels to further weed out union radicals and "weaken union leadership wherever possible."[19] It was now quite clear that SCAP was behind business, and that this support was providing management with a great deal of strength vis-a-vis the unions.[20]

The Impact of Labor and Labor-Management Relations

The policies of SCAP thus clearly impacted the labor movement. It was developments within the labor movement itself and within labor-management relations, shaped as they were by state actions, however, that most directly influenced the evolution of the Japanese model of work organization. An understanding of the "labor situation" from the early postwar years through the mid-1950s is thus necessary in order to understand why the Japanese model of work organization evolved the way it did. This section will be divided into three parts: first, the immediate postwar years during which labor strength was at its peak; second, the strike of 1953, which was the defining event in the evolution of postwar labor relations in the automobile sector; and third, the post-strike situation and the implications of the labor defeat.

Union organization blossomed in the early years after the war, and by 1949 56% of the Japanese work force had been unionized. It was during the first several years after the war that union strength was at its peak. In fact, until the early 1950s it appeared to many observers that the labor movement was stronger than management. As Kawanishi writes, "During the first five years after the war, Japan experienced a rather unique situation. For the only time in the nation's history the 'working class' was able to dominate the 'capitalist class'."[21] These years of labor strength were characterized by significant union strength in the firm and on the shop floor. Kawanishi presents four main elements of this strength. First, the foremen—in charge of production on the shop floor—became part of the union. Thus the shop-floor unit

was entirely composed of union members, and only the company executives remained part of management. Perhaps more significant, as a result of the unions' autonomy vis-a-vis management, the union foremen were able to and did advocate a position that was independent of management's and supportive of the work force. Second, workshops secured a large degree of autonomy, which further ensured the ability of workers and union foremen to elaborate positions independent of management. Third, the union managed to secure a say in personnel affairs, something which management would later come to oppose zealously. Finally, the unions were able to generate their own systems of work rules, something which, again, would eventually come under intense attack by management.[22]

Beyond the structures of workplace control which unions managed to develop in the immediate postwar years, workers also secured a number of additional gains, including a measure of job security, wage security, and "higher status within the firm." In Gordon's words, unions throughout the Japanese economy managed nearly to secure a "labor version of the Japanese employment system: guaranteed job security, an explicitly need-based seniority wage, and a significant voice in the management of factory affairs."[23]

These gains, it should be noted, were the results of strong union demands and bitter labor-management struggles engaged in throughout this period, not the product of cooperative labor-management relations. The union demands most offensive to management during these years had to do with control over shop-floor practices and labor deployment. Indeed, unions managed to win strong influence in these areas in many firms. The production-control movement was the most radical manifestation of this, but between 1945 and 1947 unions also forced management to engage in joint consultations on issues including personnel policy (e.g., job transfers, layoffs, and changes in work rules) and wages. These "management discussion councils" were incorporated into contracts during this period. In fact, two-thirds of contracts concluded by mid-1946 created and gave authority to these councils. As long as the unions were strong, the councils served labor's interest by giving the work force a voice in managerial decision making.[24]

Along with the drives to secure a union voice in managerial decision making, the immediate postwar years saw a concerted effort by the unions to ensure that the enterprise would not be the main unit of organization or bargaining. This effort met with some measure of success, albeit transitory. By 1953, 18 of Japan's largest industries had organized labor federations, and an effort was made to form a national labor federation through the unification of Sanbetsu and Sodomei. As

regards the automobile industry, Toyota, Nissan, and Isuzu joined Sanbetsu in 1946, but when Sanbetsu came under control of Communist Party members the Toyota union, reflecting an aversion to radicalism and the structural barriers to militancy it faced, withdrew from Sanbetsu and urged the other auto unions to form an automobile industry federation. Nissan and Isuzu accepted the offer, and in 1947 the All-Japan Automobile Industry Union (Zenji) was formed.[25] Within the Zenji federation, the member unions remained viable entities.

Despite the aversion to Communist radicalism displayed in the move away from Sanbetsu, the formation of Zenji marked a strengthening of the bargaining positions of all the Japanese auto unions. The auto unions' ability to develop and demand an agenda independent of management's was furthered by the existence of an industrial union which implied a loosening of the connection between the fate of the unions and the fate of the individual auto firms.

While union strength built across the late 1940s, changes in SCAP's attitude toward the labor movement and the implementation of the Dodge line eventually led to a reversal of fortunes. In 1947, when Katsuji Kawamata was sent by the Industrial Bank of Japan to improve operations at Nissan, he observed that "the union was stronger than management, and management feared [the union]."[26] When Kawamata arrived, a pattern had been established wherein management consistently acquiesced to union demands. Indeed, at Nissan, union strength reflected the general strength of the labor movement just outlined. With the change in SCAP policy and the implementation of the Dodge line, however, Kawamata felt empowered to take the measures he believed were necessary to get Nissan going again. His main strategy was to cut the work force drastically, and in 1949 Kawamata planned to fire 2,000 of Nissan's 8,500 workers—a clear managerial challenge to the union.[27]

In September 1949, Kawamata announced the firing of 1,760 workers. Union activists and radicals were specifically targeted for dismissal. Following the announcement of these firings, the Nissan union went out on strike for two months; eventually, however, management's directive was carried out and almost 25% of Nissan's work force was dismissed. The firings did not, however, cause the union to buckle, but rather served to further radicalize those remaining at Nissan, including the union's leader, Masuda Tetsuo.[28]

At Toyota, a similar series of events took place in 1949-1950. Disputes began in response to Toyota's delayed payment of wages, which the union protested. In late 1949 the union and management agreed that in exchange for a 10% wage cut, the company would stop

delaying wage payments and would not fire any workers. In spite of the agreement, wage delays continued, and the union went out on strike. Management responded to the strike by cutting wages another 10% and "requesting" resignations from over 2,000 workers. In the summer of 1950, workers protested management's actions with mass demonstrations, intermittent strikes, and "mock courts" used to "try" Toyota management.[29] Despite the strikes and labor protest, Toyota finally prevailed, and fired proportionately more workers than Nissan had in 1949.

Significantly, the strikes of 1950 were also fought over a proposed reorganization of work in the Toyota machine shop, which would initiate the development of the general Toyota system of work organization. The defeat of the Toyota workers in 1950 thus also cleared the way for the reorganization of work in the machine shop.

The Toyota workers' response to the defeat of 1950 was, however, very different from the radicalization that took place at Nissan. While Toyota fired proportionately more workers in 1950 than Nissan had in 1949, the results of the firings were quite different. As Cusumano put it:

> Since there were not many alternatives for employment in that part of Japan [Koromo], workers and residents tended to be grateful to the Toyoda family and Toyota group companies for their economic contributions to the area. After management fired a third of Toyota's workers in 1950, employees lucky enough to remain were usually more concerned with keeping their positions than with their "rights" as workers.[30]

Cusumano argues that the primary cause of the differing situations at Toyota and Nissan, perhaps surprisingly, was geography. Whereas Nissan was located in the metropolis of Tokyo, Toyota was located in Koromo, a rural countryside hundreds of miles from Tokyo. Besides farming, Toyota was the only source of employment for the 30,000 residents. In other words, Toyota was located in a quintessential company town.

Further, Toyota had created a dual internal labor market wherein "loyal workers" were made regular employees who received high wages and a promise of "lifetime employment." A large section of "temporary" workers were also employed at the firm, but remuneration for their work was much lower than the regular employees. Only

through "loyalty" to the firm could temporary employees be promoted to the ranks of the regulars. In this way Toyota management encouraged a quiescent labor force.[31] These structural conditions weakened the Toyota union in 1950, and after Zenji was defeated in 1954, the enterprise union was left to itself to defend the interests of workers.

Nonetheless, after the firings of 1949 and 1950, auto management and labor began to lock horns over a set of issues: overtime and the deployment of personnel. For management, the ability to require overtime and reassign labor at will was becoming crucial to their drive for efficiency. Moreover, control over these elements of production implied the ability to design the production system itself, and eventually would imply the ability to institute flexible production techniques. For the unions however, the ability to refuse overtime was one of the most effective levers against managerial authority, and as such was crucial to the success of union demands within the firm. That unions had won significant control over such shop-floor practices as overtime and labor deployment represented an "intolerable loss of control" to management.[32] Management needed this "control" in order to have the freedom to implement the work changes it saw as prerequisite to the success of the Japanese auto industry. It was, in the end, over this issue of control that the strike of 1953 would be fought.[33]

By 1953, however, wage negotiations had become the main point of contention. In the wage negotiations of that year, Zenji was asking for a sliding wage scale based on seniority and a set base wage for new employees. Under the Zenji plan, wages would rise ¥1000 per year. Nissan, however, rejected this plan, and in response to this rejection a work slowdown was instituted. As a last provocation before the strike, management at Nissan ordered that section chiefs, previously part of the union, become part of management. The section chiefs were very important members of the shop-floor work group, responsible for transmitting managerial initiatives to the shop floor. The inclusion of the section chiefs into the managerial fold therefore represented another move by management to retake control of the shop floor, and to ensure themselves the ability to implement changes in the organization of work.[34]

The strike of 1953, though perhaps immediately provoked by a struggle over wages, represented a struggle for control of the production process. The unions and management both understood that such things as the power to control overtime and labor deployment really represented the power to control the way in which work was carried out. However, perhaps of equal importance to the fight for control over the

work process was that the fate of Japan's industrial unions was also at stake in the strike of 1953. In order to have the autonomy and the strength to influence effectively decisions regarding the organization of work, a viable industrial union federation was needed. Striking labor leaders were thus committed to building a strong industrial union movement. In contrast, management understood that their ability to control the work process depended on the promulgation of enterprise unionism and thus sought, through the strike of 1953, to defeat the industrial union movement.[35] As Cusumano put it, the 1953 strike was "a contest between organized labor, with the goal of joining workers in the same industry, and Japanese management . . . who sought to reduce the power of labor federations created after World War Two."[36] The 1953 strike, in determining the future of labor organization in the Japanese auto industry, would also determine who would control the organization of work.

By 1953 both camps felt strong enough to test the other. While it was the union that went out on strike, it was clear enough that the employers were provoking the confrontation as forcefully as labor was willing to engage in it. Approaching the strike, the Japanese unions had a fairly developed strategy. The strategy was to identify the leading firm in a sector and launch an attack there, the rationale being that if the leading firm were to agree to the union's terms, then the other firms would follow. As Nissan appeared the leading firm in the auto industry in 1953, it was chosen as the union's target. However, other factors went into the selection of Nissan as the primary target for the strike. First, the location of Toyota in a classic company town, along with its dual internal labor market, had made the Toyota union relatively unwilling to directly oppose management. Further, while the Red Purge of 1950, along with the selective firings of 1949 and 1950 had succeeded in de-radicalizing the auto unions, the Nissan union under the leadership of Masuda Tetsuo remained strong.[37]

While Nissan may have been the best target for the unions anyway, the fact that the struggle in 1953 primarily took place there was also the result of the employers' strategy. As the unions wanted to target Nissan, the employers had their reasons for targeting the Nissan union. First, this union was by far the strongest of the Japanese auto unions, and Masuda was at the head of the drive to develop a strong industrial union for Japanese auto. Thus, by defeating the Nissan union, the employers would not only bust the strongest member of Zenji, but would begin the process of destroying Zenji itself.

A primary plank in the employers' strategy was to isolate the Nissan union from its Zenji affiliates at Toyota and Isuzu. To achieve

this goal, Nissan management secured the cooperation of executives at Toyota and Isuzu, as well as that of Nikkeiren officials. As a result of negotiations with Nissan executives, Toyota management thus reached a settlement with its union on August 4, and Isuzu reached settlement on August 5. As another part of the strategy to destroy the Nissan union, Nikkeiren arranged a deal with Toyota and Isuzu which guaranteed Nissan that neither Toyota nor Isuzu would take Nissan's market share during the strike. This, of course, took away one of the union's main weapons and thus strengthened management against the Nissan union.[38] In addition, the Industrial Bank of Japan (IBJ) and the Fuji Bank agreed to loan ¥540,000,000 to Nissan during the strike to keep the company alive and to assist its efforts to dismantle the powerful Nissan union. Beyond simply busting the Masuda union, management also hoped to replace the original, militant union with a second union more cooperative with management's initiatives. This was a sure-fire way to regain control of the shop floor.

Detailed accounts of the strike are given in *The Japanese Automobile Industry* and in Halberstam's *The Reckoning*, and here I summarize the main events as concisely as possible. On July 11, 1953, the union ordered unlimited strikes, and production was completely halted. On August 5, 1953, management locked the Masuda union out of the factories, and ordered the erection of physical barricades to secure the lock-out. When employees attempted to reenter the buildings the police were called in, and several union leaders, including Masuda himself, were arrested. Following the arrests, Nissan management made a crucial move: they refused to bargain with the Masuda union. This was perhaps the most effective step management could have taken in light of their strategy to replace the Masuda union with a second union. According to Okumura (author of a 1954 book on auto manufacturing), "Management simply disappeared. Company executives set up an undercover office and moved frequently. When the union tried to resume the negotiations, it had no one to negotiate with."[39]

While it was management's decision not to negotiate with Masuda's union, it is important to understand why Nissan had the capacity to refuse these negotiations despite the fact that production had been completely halted. The company not only had ¥540,000,000 in loans to support itself during the strike, it also had assurances that neither of its competitors were going to infringe on its market share. Thus, while the Masuda union was strong, management had assembled a nearly impenetrable defensive apparatus. With management refusing to negotiate, and the police protecting the factory, the Masuda union could do nothing more than remain on strike. While management had

the IBJ behind it, however, union members were without a wage. Considering the dire condition of Japan's economy during these postwar years, management could better survive the strike than could the union.

As the strike continued, management began encouraging the development of a second, collaborative union. For several years before the strike, a group of white-collar union members under the leadership of Miyake Masaru had been expressing dissent with Masuda's confrontational policies. In order to best serve everyone's interests, they argued, the union needed to support the company. IBJ representative Kawamata and Nissan management saw Masaru's dissident group as the key to developing a second union. On August 30, 506 workers gathered in Tokyo to form this new union, the Nissan Motor Labor Union. The slogans displayed at this conference indicate the stance the new union was to take toward management: "Those who love the union love the company," "Fight for wages that promote the desire to work," and "Guarantee a wage based on productivity increases."[40]

Contrary to the Nissan company history which claims that this new union voiced the discontent of the mass of workers previously under Masuda, the August 30 meeting followed the *failure* of a no-confidence vote designed to oust the leaders of the first union. Again contrary to company claims that the new union was representative of the "average" Nissan worker, most of the 506 employees who gathered to form the new union were white-collar, college-educated employees. The second union held its mass meeting, with police protection, against the protests of the mass of workers who remained committed to Masuda and the original union. At the time that the Nissan Motor Labor Union was forming, 86% of union members wanted to continue the strike, while only 11% openly disapproved.[41]

Despite the clear support shown by the vast majority of Nissan employees for Masuda's union tactics, the second union was formed. Immediately, management opened negotiations with the second union. What perhaps ultimately turned the tide in the 1953 strike was management's offer to allow those who joined the second union to return to work at 60% of previous wages, despite the fact that the factory was completely shut down. Masaru and his associates, offering wages to workers who had been out of work for several months, began to attract a new membership. By the end of September the new union had greater than 3,000 members and had negotiated a new labor contract with management.[42]

Masuda realized that he was defeated. The new union was promising management exactly what it wanted—control over the organization of work and the deployment of the work force. Moreover,

the new union, thanks to the loans from the IBJ, was providing Nissan workers what Masuda's union could not provide—income. Realizing finally that he was "fighting against a well organized and well financed foe—indeed, against the full force of postwar Japanese capitalism" Masuda capitulated to managerial demands and sent his union back to work. Once operations at Nissan started up again, Masuda supporters were given the worst jobs or forced to leave. Masuda and the other union leaders were fired and, by the end of 1953, management, as they had set out to do, had won complete control of the factory floor through the new union.

There were several immediate implications of the defeat of the Masuda union and its replacement by the second union at Nissan, including a 16% wage reduction and the implementation of the *sagyocho* foremen system which incorporated foremen into management, and gave them much greater control over workers on the shop floor. Its longer term implications, however, would clearly shape the evolution of the Japanese model of work organization.[43] The 1953 labor defeat had marked the defeat of Zenji and thus the defeat of the industrial union movement in the Japanese auto industry. When workers at Nissan left Masuda's union to join the second union, they also left Zenji, marking the dissolution of Zenji's most powerful affiliate. Moreover, Zenji had depleted its financial resources in its attempt to provide support to the striking Nissan workers. Finally, union leaders acknowledged that the failure to keep the Nissan, Toyota, and Isuzu unions united during the strike indicated that Zenji was no longer an effective representative force for the autoworkers. Faced with financial and representational crisis, Zenji was officially dissolved in December 1954.[44]

As Cusumano put it, the dissolution of Zenji "left the Japanese automobile industry with nothing but company unions," which became the organizing and bargaining unit of the entire auto sector.[45] The triumph of the enterprise union over the industrial union carried serious implications for Japanese autoworkers across the industry, since an enterprise union is based entirely within one firm and the union's workers are dependent for their well-being on the success of that firm. Any actions taken by the union which disrupt the productivity or threaten the profitability of the firm, also threaten the workers who form the union. As such, all strikes, work slowdowns, etc., become double-edged swords: while they may be useful to achieve union demands, they jeopardize worker interests in the process. Thus in any system of enterprise unionism, unions will more than likely cooperate and share the same goals with management. With regard to wages and

benefits, the good of the firm most realistically does come to represent the good of the union.

Not only are enterprise unions inherently weak, but the specific form that enterprise unionism took in Japan implied further weakness of unions and workers vis-a-vis management. As discussed, the enterprise unions in the immediate postwar years did maintain a level of autonomy vis-a-vis management, and were thereby able to develop an independent agenda for the organization and operation of their firms. At Nissan after the defeat in 1953, and the institution of the "second union," this autonomy was lost. Voting for union officials was done under the surveillance of supervisors, ensuring that union posts were filled with people loyal to the firm.[46] The Toyota enterprise union, for the reasons outlined above, was especially reluctant to formulate any agenda which conflicted with managerial goals. Without the industrial union behind them, the Japanese auto unions were doomed to a weakness which implied many things for the future of the Japanese automobile industry.

Most importantly, the defeat of the industrial union movement in 1953 and the rise of the managerially dominated enterprise union meant that management was given a free hand in shaping the organization of the shop floor. Following the end of the strike, and the defeat of the industrial union movement, it was clear that the auto unions were collaborating with management in the institution of managerial initiatives.[47]

The Impact of the Economic Environment

An investigation of the Japanese economy in the late 1940s and early 1950s explains the conditions that induced management to form the specific organization of work that ultimately developed. With regard to Toyota, Cusumano states that "to a large degree, the changes that Toyota made were 'evolutionary' adaptations to the circumstances surrounding the company and to domestic market needs."[48] One of the most important of these "circumstances" was the fact that while Japanese auto production in the early 1950s was based on American production technology, which was designed to manufacture standardized goods for mass markets, the Japanese market was much smaller than the American market. Because mass markets did not exist in Japan, Japanese auto firms had to adjust production methods to the needs of a more limited market. In 1950, for example, the Japanese auto industry produced only 30,000 autos—the equivalent of one and one half days' production in the United States.[49]

It was, however, the conjunction of these limited markets with the demand for a highly diversified product line that ultimately shaped the decisions regarding production and work organization. Although Nissan had only eight factories in 1951, it was producing large trucks, small trucks, small cars, and buses. In the early 1950s, Toyota faced the same demand for different car and truck models. Korean War orders, for example, forced Toyota to manufacture a variety of new vehicle types in addition to the passenger car models the company was trying to develop. Rather than producing a single product for mass markets, as was demanded in Fordist economies, Japanese managers were thus forced by their particular economic environment to produce a variety of vehicle models in small quantities. As a result:

> All Japanese automakers became more efficient because they had to modify American mass production techniques to produce in smaller numbers. Volume requirements were extremely low in Japan during the 1950s, yet the domestic market called for an increasing number of different car and truck models.[50]

The need to produce a diversified product line in small quantities forced the Japanese auto firms to develop flexible production strategies.

Beyond the demands imposed by small market size and production capacity, in conjunction with demand for a variety of automobile models, an early attempt to penetrate the U.S. market also shaped the future production strategy, and subsequently the design of work changes of the Japanese auto industry. Japanese auto firms first attempted to export to U.S. markets in the 1950s, but although labor costs in Japan were lower than those in the U.S., the fiscal strength of the larger U.S. automakers allowed them to undersell the Japanese firms. Even if it meant selling for a while at a loss, the U.S. firms were able to drive the Japanese from the U.S. market.[51] While this represented a setback for Japanese auto at the time, it interests us here because of the lesson this export failure taught the Japanese firms. Unable to compete in international markets on the basis of price, and driven to those markets by a limited domestic demand[52], the Japanese auto firms learned that they needed to compete on product grounds.

This scenario went beyond simply encouraging the Japanese to introduce a new model, or to seek a "niche market" (i.e., compact cars), however, for just as the American makers could undersell the smaller Japanese firms in the standard car market, the Big Three could develop

similar niche cars and undersell the Japanese in these markets. The implications of this were critical. In Friedman's words, "Many influential Japanese auto strategists drew the lesson that only by *continuously differentiating* their products could they avoid price pressures from U.S. firms."[53] From the experience of early failure in export markets, then, the Japanese firms understood their need to develop a production process capable of continuous product change. Again, this called for flexibility.

A third condition of the economic environment confronting Japanese automakers in the early 1950s was a crisis of costs and quality. During the immediate postwar years the costs of basic inputs were so high that Japanese cars were not competitive with imports from the U.S. and Western Europe. The quality of Japanese autos was likewise totally uncompetitive in the early 1950s. However, in order to meet the demands of SCAP standards in the 1950s and the standards of consumers in the 1960s, great efforts had to be made to improve quality and to lower costs. At Toyota especially, this drive to solve the crisis of costs and quality was carried out through reforms on the shop floor.

Ohno Taiichi was most responsible for shop-floor reforms at Toyota and was charged, by president Toyoda in 1948, with the task of eliminating all waste from the production process. Through this elimination of waste, cost control was to be secured.[54] Ohno's first strategy was to eradicate all "idle time." He instituted the use of standard time and motion studies in an attempt to remove all unnecessary movements from the work process. "Excess" workers would then be removed from the production line. Beyond this, however, Ohno implemented the distinction between the "operating time of a machine," and the "working time of its operator." The status quo procedure, typical in Fordist auto firms, was that workers were considered working while their machines were in operation, despite the fact that they might not be actively engaged in any motions themselves. In Ohno's system, if while one machine was in operation a worker was left idle, s/he was expected to engage in another task, usually on another machine.[55] While this clearly increased the intensity of work, it also required flexibility from the production line work force.

Beyond the reduction of idle time, Ohno's drive to eliminate waste brought him to attack the level of inventories held in the production process. One of the major flaws Ohno saw in the American production strategy, implicit in the American technology Toyota had imported, was the creation of huge inventories through large lot production. These inventories were very costly for the firm, especially for a firm as small as Toyota. In response, Ohno developed a production system that did

not require the use of inventories. The Just-in-Time production process
that resulted was to be a primary element in the new form of work
organization, and would have serious consequences for the workers
employed under its dictates. It was the drive to reduce costs, brought on
by the cost crisis of the early 1950s that predicated the development of
this production system.

Finally, while Ohno's reforms in the area of "idle time" and
inventory control worked to solve the crisis of costs, other reforms were
implemented in response to the crisis of quality. As noted, in response
to SCAP quality standards in the 1950s, Japanese auto firms began to
implement quality control programs. The nature of these quality control
programs was influenced by another condition of the Japanese economy:
imported technology and the resultant "technically ignorant"
management encouraged the devolution of quality control responsibility
to workers on the shop floor.[56]

While it is hopefully clear how management secured the
prerogative to implement the production changes it deemed necessary,
why these changes were carried out through shop-floor reform (as
opposed to, for example, technological changes) may still be unclear.
Amsden argues that late industrializers such as Japan lack the
competitive asset of "being able to monopolize an original
technology."[57] As a result, firms in late industrializing countries must
find an alternative way to become competitive in global markets. The
most common solution is through developing alternative systems of
work organization. In Amsden's words:

> Different modes of industrializing, one with and one
> without original technology, are associated with
> differences in what may be termed the firm's strategic
> focus. The corporate office, inclusive of research and
> development functions, tends to be the strategic focus
> of companies that compete on the basis of innovation
> . . . By contrast, the shop floor tends to be the
> strategic focus of firms that compete on the basis of
> making borrowed technology work. Because products
> similar to those of the company are internationally
> available, the strategic focus is necessarily to be
> found where the achievement of incremental, yet
> cumulative, improvements in productivity and
> product specification occur, and therefore enhance
> competitiveness.[58]

This helps shed light on why the Japanese chose to fight their competitive battles on the shop floor.

3. CONCLUSION

The factors which led to the establishment of the Japanese model of work organization have been detailed in this chapter. The conditions which led to the development of this model impacted the form which the new system ultimately took. The Japanese model of work organization evolved out of the interaction between the defeat of the independent labor movement in the early 1950s and a series of economic conditions particular to Japan during this period. Thus while the post-Fordist world economy resembles the Japanese economic environment of the 1950s and for this reason calls forth a model of flexible work organization similar to that developed in Japan in the 1950s, post-Fordism alone cannot account for either the development or the success of this model. The development and success of the Japanese model depends not on the crisis of Fordism and the rise of post-Fordist international markets, but on the subordination of labor to the demands of management.

NOTES

1. Taiichi Ohno, "How the Toyota Production was Created," in Kazuo Sato and Yasuo Hoshino, eds., *The Anatomy of Japanese Business* (Armonk, NY: ME Sharpe, Inc., 1984), p. 197.

2. Michael Cusumano, *The Japanese Automobile Industry: Technology and Management at Nissan and Toyota* (Cambridge: Harvard University Press, 1985), pp. 265 and 279.

3. Cusumano, pp. 281, 284 and 274. All of these terms, including Just-in-Time, kanban, mixed assembly, and small lot production, will be explained in Chapter Five. Here, it is only important to note that these are the central components of the Japanese model of work organization under investigation, and that they had been developed by the 1960s.

4. Alice H. Amsden, "Third World Industrialization: 'Global Fordism' or a New Model?" *New Left Review* 182 (July-August 1990), p. 10.

5. Andrew Gordon, *The Evolution of Labor Relations in Japan: Heavy Industry, 1853-1955* (Cambridge: Harvard University Press, 1985), p. 330.

6. Gordon, p. 331.

7. Cusumano, p. 138.

8. Significantly, for reasons outlined below, while the early Toyota enterprise union was able to formulate and voice independent demands in the immediate postwar years, this enterprise union was never radicalized, and faced structural barriers to increasing the militancy of its demands. For this reason, as I'll argue, the defeat of the industrial union movement was especially crippling to an independent, and strong, labor voice at Toyota.

9. David Halberstam, *The Reckoning* (New York: William Morrow and Company, Inc., 1986), p. 116.

10. Gordon, p. 332.

11. Halberstam, p. 122.

12. Gordon, p. 336.

13. Halberstam, p. 122; Gordon, p. 336..

14. Gordon, pp. 332-333.

15. Joe Moore, "Production Control: Workers' Control in Early Postwar Japan," in E. Patricia Tsurumi, ed, *The Other Japan: Postwar Realities* (Armonk, NY: M.E. Sharpe, Inc., 1988), p. 16. As I will argue, the type of enterprise unions which came to dominate Japanese auto, were not the militant, independent type enterprise unions of the immediate postwar years.

16. Gordon, pp. 367-368.

17. Halberstam, p. 123; Gordon, pp. 332 and 371.

18. Gordon, p. 332.

19. Gordon, p. 337. Also see Halberstam, pp. 125 and 129; Gordon, p. 336.

20. While these developments mark the most significant impact of the state on the development of the new model of work organization, a word should be said regarding the relations between the government and business which would later become so crucial to the Japanese economy, and to academic writing on Japanese political economy. In the early 1950s the strong state interventionist model did begin to emerge, and MITI targeted the automobile industry as the "infant industry" which would become the core of its industrial policy. MITI first encouraged Japanese auto firms to enter into "tie-ups," or mergers, with American and European firms. While initially these led to import domination of Japanese markets, the ultimate goal of the tie-ups was the transfer of

technology and production techniques to allow total domestication of production. But by the mid-1950s, MITI and other governmental agencies were taking a more direct role in fostering the Japanese auto industry by providing capital and technological assistance to the auto firms. (See T.J. Pempel, *Policy and Politics in Japan: Creative Conservatism* (Philadelphia: Temple University Press, 1982), p. 59.) In May of 1955, MITI began the "Citizens' Car Project" to support the development of a passenger car industry, and in 1956 the Provisional Act for the Promotion of Machinery Industries provided low-interest loans to auto firms which renovated production facilities. This act also gave MITI a role in hastening the "rationalization of production." (Konosuke Odaka, Keinosuke Ono, and Fumihiko Adachi, *The Automobile Industry in Japan: A Study of Ancillary Firm Development* (Oxford: Kinokuniya Company LTD, Oxford University Press, 1988), pp. 46-47.) Thus, although not central to the argument here, strong state-business relations were already manifest in early postwar Japan.

21. Hirosuke Kawanishi, *Enterprise Unionism in Japan*. (New York: Kegan Paul International, 1992), p. 100.

22. Kawanishi, pp. 104-107.

23. Gordon, p. 330.

24. Gordon, pp. 345-346.

25. Cusumano, p. 144.

26. Halberstam, pp. 139-140.

27. Halberstam, p. 140.

28. Gordon, p. 390; Halberstam, p. 141.

29. Satoshi Kamata, *Japan in the Passing Lane: An Insider's Account of Life in a Japanese Auto Factory*, Translated and edited by Tatsuru Akimoto (New York: Pantheon books, 1982), p. 9.

30. Cusumano, p. 180-181.

31. Cusumano, p. 183.

32. Berggren, *Alternatives to Lean Production*. Op cit., p. 24.

33. Berggren, p. 25; Halberstam, p. 151; Cusumano, p. 151.

34. Halberstam, pp. 154-155.

35. Through the strike of 1953 management also sought to weaken the enterprise unions that had formed in the immediate postwar years. This was more significant at Nissan than at Toyota, however, due to the structural weakness of the Toyota enterprise union. With regard to the Toyota union and Toyota workers, the fate of the industrial union movement was the most important element of the '53 strike.

36. Cusumano, p. 143.

37. Halberstam, p. 131-132.

38. Halberstam, p. 168.
39. Cusumano, p. 152.
40. Cusumano, p. 156.
41. Cusumano, pp. 155-157.
42. Halberstam, pp. 171 and 182.
43. Cusumano, p. 160. Not only were foremen given power over other workers, but they had the responsibility to assess workers for promotions, raises transfers and training. (See Shigeyoshi Tokunaga, "A Marxist Interpretation of Japanese Industrial Relations, with Special Reference to Large Private Enterprises," in Taishiro Shirai, ed. *Contemporary Industrial Relations in Japan* (Madison: University of Wisconsin Press, 1983), p. 316.)
44. Cusumano, pp. 163 and 157. The defeat of Japanese labor in 1953 was in clear contrast to the increasing power of the auto unions in the United States and Western Europe during the 1950s and 1960s. As regards Japan's place in the Fordism/Crisis of Fordism debate, this development clearly marks a departure from the pattern of the Fordist countries. As we will see, it was this defeat of the independent labor movement, not the crisis of Fordism, which paved the way for the development of the Japanese model of work organization.
45. Cusumano, p. 163.
46. See Yamamoto Kiyoshi, "Labor-Management Relations at Nissan Motor Co., Ltd. (Datsun)," *Annals of the Institute of Social Science* No. 21. (Tokyo: University of Tokyo, 1980), p. 7. Also Tokunaga, p. 321.
47. "The unions became little more than an administrative arm of management in the area of personnel affairs." (Kawanishi. pp. 117 and 112.) At Nissan, the new union granted management the right to freely implement "productivity increase programs and other measures to ensure the future prosperity of the firm," in exchange for a promise of job guarantees for regular employees. Cusumano, p. 165.

While management's ability to control the organization of work was the most important result of the labor struggles of the early 1950s, there were several other important implications. Among these was the "critical lack" of a social force capable of securing a welfare policy. (See Berggren, p. 25.) This of course adds another dimension upon which we may deem Japan a "non-Fordist" state. Second, in order to avoid a repetition of the labor militance they experienced in the early fifties, Japanese firms made several important decisions. One, rather than risking the repercussions of more mass layoffs Japanese management was prone to introduce guarantees of job security in the coming years.

(See Gordon, pp. 390-400.) Two, partly in order to avoid the chance of a revitalized labor movement, auto firms began outsourcing work to ancillary firms rather than following the American model of vertical integration. (See Michael J. Smitka, *Competitive Ties: Subcontracting in the Japanese Automotive Industry* (New York: Columbia University Press, 1991), pp. 6-7.) While these implications are all important, they do not call for further explication here.

48. Cusumano, p. 266.
49. Cusumano, p. 266.
50. Cusumano, p. 221 and 266.
51. David Friedman, *The Misunderstood Miracle: Industrial Development and Political Change in Japan* (Ithaca: Cornell University Press, 1988), p. 12.
52. As was pointed out in Chapter One, one element of the Fordist economy is production directed primarily towards domestic markets. This fact allowed the establishment of demand stabilization mechanisms through the domestic economy and through national government policies to be effective. The fact of the limited domestic market in Japan not only implies the non-Fordist need to direct sales overseas, but also implies that were Fordist demand stabilization policies attempted on the domestic level, their effectiveness would have been limited. In another way, then, the Japanese case clearly departs from the Fordist paradigm.
53. Friedman, p. 12. Emphasis added.
54. The reforms were begun in the machine shop which Ohno directed, and were subsequently spread throughout Toyota. The strike defeat of 1950, as noted above, was instrumental in giving Ohno, and management in general, the ability to institute these reforms in the machine shop. The more general defeat of industrial unionism in 1953 left the Toyota workers with only an ineffectual enterprise union and thus no mechanism for opposing the spread of these reforms throughout Toyota.
55. Cusumano, pp. 271-273.
56. Amsden, p. 12.
57. Amsden, p. 5.
58. Amsden, p. 17.

Chapter Four
The Preconditions for Work Changes in the Swedish Automobile Industry

As with the Japanese case, the redesign of work in the Swedish auto industry evolved out of the interaction between a set of economic conditions which demanded flexible production and the strength of organized labor—again, conditioned by state policies. However, while the Japanese system of work organization did not evolve out of a challenged Fordist economic regime, the Swedish model does. Moreover, and perhaps more importantly, the changes implemented in Japan were implemented by a management unfettered by labor demands or an independent labor agenda. In contrast, the Swedish changes were a result of labor strength, in an economic environment shaped by that strength. As such, labor's voice was incorporated into the design of these changes.

1. FORDISM IN SWEDEN: THE "HISTORICAL COMPROMISE" AND THE REHN-MEIDNER MODEL

The Pre-War Years

In the Swedish version of Fordism, the three major social actors—labor, business, and the state—had their inceptions well before the Fordist years. By the end of the nineteenth century there were already thirty-two national unions in Sweden. By 1907, 40% of men in the core industrial sectors had unionized, and a confederation of national unions had formed in 1898. Known as The Swedish Trade Union Confederation (*Landsorganisationen i Sverige*, or LO), this confederation would play a dominant role in Swedish political economy and industrial relations throughout the twentieth century. While the Japanese labor movement has been defined by enterprise unionism, the Swedish labor movement has been characterized by industrial unions

and high rates of organization. At the 1912 LO Congress, industrial unionism was made the primary organizational unit for affiliated unions, and by the beginning of the Fordist years, 78% of all LO unions were industrial unions, the rest being craft or mixed industrial/craft unions.[1]

LO's partner in the Social Democratic movement, the Social Democratic Labor Party (*Socialdeomkratiska Arbetareparti*, or the SAP), was also formed well before the Fordist years, and would play a similarly crucial role throughout the twentieth century. Indeed, the SAP and LO were linked from inception, and electoral support for the SAP has been consistently located within the working class. The SAP was a major political force by the turn of the century, and with the extension of the franchise in 1909 the SAP became the largest party in the second chamber of the Riksdag. In the earliest days of the party's existence, the SAP called for a transformation of society through the abolishment of private ownership of the means of production, as indicated by the party program of 1897: "The Social Democratic Party differs from other political parties by wanting to totally restructure the economic organization of bourgeois society."[2] In addition to a strong labor movement, the Social Democratic movement was thus equipped with a powerful political party aimed at the transformation of society.[3]

Swedish capital formed its own powerful confederation in the first years of the twentieth century. A 1902 nationwide strike for suffrage, which ultimately led to the granting of universal voting rights in Sweden, also motivated Swedish employers to unify in order to address the growing strength of the labor movement, clearly exhibited during this strike. Thus to "achieve unified action among employers in the face of the rapidly growing working class movement," the Swedish Employer's Confederation (*Svenska Arbetasgivareföreningen*, or SAF) was formed.[4] While this confederation quickly became the representative voice for nearly all of Swedish capital, SAF's approach to industrial relations in the early years was distinct from many Swedish firms of the time. Rather than attempting to bust the highly organized and centralized unions, the SAF approach was to recognize unions' right to organize while demanding in return union recognition of management's "right to manage."

This was the strategy of union-management relations that most suited the situation at the turn of the century. While not strong enough to demand ownership of private capital, the Swedish labor movement was strong enough to defeat a campaign of union busting. Reflecting the position of both the unions and management, then, in 1906 LO and SAF agreed to the December Compromise. An early predecessor of the

famous Saltsjöbaden agreement of 1938, the December Compromise granted workers the right to organize into unions without employer interference, and granted management the right to perform all managerial functions, including hiring and firing, and designing the organization of work.[5]

The December Compromise was a first step in the institutionalization of Swedish industrial relations and in the stabilization of Swedish political economy that predicted the situation in the Fordist years. Following the Compromise, however, several decades of labor-management strife ensued, and it was not until 1938, when LO and SAF signed onto the Saltsjöbaden Basic Agreement, that the well known "historical compromise" between Swedish labor and business emerged. Saltsjöbaden was a product of SAF and LO preference for negotiations over labor market legislation which had taken shape by the late 1930s. LO was concerned with securing power over the strike weapon and with averting the imposition of legal limits on its use. SAF was equally happy to avoid government intervention in the labor market because by the late 1930s it was clear that the SAP was securely in power and not likely to legislate on SAF's behalf. As a result, the two confederations agreed that they would settle all industrial-relations issues through centralized collective bargaining and not rely on state intervention in the labor market.

Of the agreements made at Saltsjöbaden, the most important simply reinforced those made in the December Compromise: workers were to have the right to organize into unions, and management was to have the right to manage. This second provision was written into SAF's constitution as §32. At Saltsjöbaden, the unions also agreed not to strike during the length of a contract, but to bargain collectively with SAF over all issues of conflict, including wage disputes.[6] Again, however, management's right to hire and fire and to design and organize work were not within the scope of these collective negotiations according to §32 of the SAF constitution.

In the interwar years an institutionalized system of industrial relations was thereby established which later would fit perfectly into Sweden's version of Fordism. With the stabilization of political power in the hands of the SAP, and following the experience of the Great Depression, the party began to formulate another backbone of Swedish Fordism: a Keynesian demand management program designed to end unemployment and stimulate demand. In order to spur economic recovery, public works projects in which workers were paid normal wage rates were instituted, and redistributive economic policies were implemented.[7] With the implementation of these programs the SAP's

power was stabilized, and between this time and 1976, the Social Democrats remained in control of the Swedish government.

In the context of political control by the country's left-wing party, LO came to understand its own interests as tied to the continued electoral success of the SAP. This implied that because the success of the party was influenced by the success of the economy, LO had to concern itself with the health of the general Swedish economy. In the labor market, this served to strengthen the restriction on strikes that Saltsjöbaden had instituted.

The Postwar Years

Following the experience of the war years, a joint LO-SAP committee prepared the "Postwar Program of Swedish Labor" which outlined the goals of the social-democratic movement for the postwar years. Predicting the program that would take shape in the late 1960s, this Program called for state control of investment and extensive labor control over workplace planning.[8] While the SAP was strong at this time, it was not however strong enough to secure so radical a program, especially as it was still reliant on parliamentary support from the more centrist Farmers' Party. As such, the Postwar Program was abandoned, to be re-instituted as LO-SAP policy in the late 1960s. These earlier postwar years came to be defined by a different set of priorities.

As noted, LO had come to understand its own interests as tied to the electoral success of the SAP. In a country defined by capitalist markets and electoral politics such as Sweden, the success of the economy and the success of the party in control of the government are intimately linked. As such, the SAP could only remain in power—and LO maintain this politically powerful ally—so long as the economy functioned successfully. LO therefore began to avoid taking measures which would harm economic performance, clearly a significant policy and strategy consideration for a labor union as strong as LO. We've seen already that LO began restricting strike actions as early as the 1930s, and this continued through to the postwar years. Regard for general economic health also had serious effects on wage negotiations, as will be discussed below.

But beyond the specific ways in which LO acted to protect the economy and thereby the SAP's power, the relationship between the union and the party implied something important about the organization of LO. In order to facilitate LO's function of protecting the SAP's electoral success, the central LO administration had to have control over both wage negotiations and the strike activities of affiliated

unions. A 1941 change in LO's constitution forbid any affiliated union from striking without the approval of the LO executive body. Further, through the development of the Rehn-Meidner model of political economy, LO gained centralized control over wage negotiations in Swedish industry. This centralization provided Sweden with its variant of the Fordist wage bargaining structure, as wages could be pegged to productivity levels and thereby sufficient demand stimulated through LO-SAF negotiations. However, this centralization of control later provided impetus for a rank-and-file rebellion which ultimately contributed to the drive for industrial democracy and the evolution of work changes in the Swedish auto industry, as I will show.

But industrial democracy and the organization of the workplace were not important issues for the Social Democratic movement in the early postwar period. At the end of World War II, there was interest in participation reforms, and works councils were established by LO-SAF agreement. However, these councils were given consultative functions only, and were peripheral to the main focus of the movement.[9] Evolving out of the experience of the Depression, and more particularly out of the economic-political collaboration of LO and the SAP, the primary goal of the Social Democratic movement in the postwar years became increasing productivity growth and achieving the "best possible production."[10]

The consequences for unions were twofold, and reflective of the typical Fordist compromise discussed in Chapter One. First, through increasing levels of production, workers benefited with higher wages and higher levels of employment. In achieving these productivity gains, however, the Swedish unions had to acquiesce to a "rationalization drive, including time studies and assembly line production."[11] As long as production and economic success remained the goals of LO and the SAP, this acquiescence was acceptable to both the union and the party. By the late 1960s, however, this trade-off proved another element in the rank-and-file rebellion from LO, and another impetus towards industrial democracy and work reorganization.

Because a Social Democratic movement was setting the policy agenda of the postwar years, however, production goals were tempered with the demand for full-employment. Indeed, Korpi terms full-employment the "cornerstone" of the postwar policy strategy.[12] This dual commitment, and the success of the full-employment policies, led to a new economic dilemma for Sweden. While the problem in the early 1930s had been lack of demand and unemployment, the problem in the 1950s quickly became restraining the inflation which accompanied full-employment. Price stability was crucial to all Fordist economies, as

we've seen. Inflation, however, was an especially tricky problem for the Social Democrats because price increases were often the result of wage increases, and thus controlling inflation often implied restricting wage growth. Dependent on LO and the working class for the mass of their electoral support, inflation was a serious issue for the SAP.[13]

In mid-1940s, Swedish inflation was rising largely as a result of an 8% rise in manufacturing wages and, in response, the government appealed to LO to freeze wages in 1948 and 1949. LO agreed, and a temporary solution was found. With the Korean War boom, however, wages and prices erupted again, and again the government called for a wage freeze. This time, however, LO refused. The union had been willing to accept the wage freeze as a one-time response to check inflation, but was not willing to use wage restraint as the consistent policy to combat inflation. The SAP, in turn, could not force wage restraint on the unions without jeopardizing electoral support. In order to maintain adherence to the goal of high economic growth and full-employment while restricting inflation, another solution was needed.

In their 1951 report "Trade Unions and Full-Employment" LO proposed such a solution in the form of the "Rehn-Meidner model." It was this model which defined Social Democratic policy and the Swedish political economy throughout the postwar period, until a change was forced in the late 1960s. When proposing the Rehn-Meidner model, LO had to keep three goals in mind: economic growth, full-employment, and low inflation. The basic tenet of the model was full-employment for all Swedish workers, *but not in those industries which were least competitive at the time*. This variant of full-employment was to be facilitated by a fiscal policy imposed by the state in conjunction with wage bargaining based on the principle of wage solidarity (see below).

The state's role was to provide a restrictive fiscal policy that kept demand high enough to support economic growth, but not so high as to induce inflation, through the institution of an increased sales tax. By increasing the sales tax, business' ability to compensate for higher wage costs with higher prices was restricted. When coordinated with the unions' solidaristic wage policy, this sales tax squeezed profits in the least profitable firms, thus contributing to the structural rationalization of industry and thereby to the goal of economic growth.

The government also contributed to full-employment through a series of active labor-market policies (including retraining and relocation programs, in addition to public works projects and unemployment relief which were designed as temporary measures) which ensured that workers displaced during structural economic adjustment would find new jobs. Rather than increasing the general level of demand in order to

compensate for unemployment caused by structural adjustment—a potentially inflationary policy—government policy was restricted to those workers actually displaced. In this manner, economic growth and full-employment could be balanced with stable prices.

The real heart of the Rehn-Meidner model, however, came with the union's solidaristic wage policy which dictated that all Swedish workers would receive equal pay for equal work, and that wages would not be determined by the profitability of individual firms. Wage rates were set across entire industries and applied to the most and least profitable firms equally. Less competitive firms and sectors would thus be driven out of business by wage rates they could not afford to pay. At the same time, the most competitive firms in the most competitive sectors would pay lower wage rates than those they could afford, providing them excess profits and capital for investment.

While the setting of appropriate wage rates proved a difficult element in the union strategy—as rates had to be set high enough to discourage wage drift in the profitable firms but not too high as to restrict the availability of investment capital in these firms—through this wage policy, competitive firms in competitive sectors grew as uncompetitive firms in uncompetitive sectors were closed. Those workers who faced unemployment found jobs in the expanding sectors of the economy after retraining and relocation was provided by the state. In this way, the Swedish economy was rationalized and expanded, while full-employment was ensured. Moreover, the solidaristic wage policy contributed to the battle against inflation by setting non-inflationary rates of wage growth and reducing union rivalry over wages, thereby eliminating the wage-wage inflationary spiral.[14]

Although centralization of union control to the confederal level had already been necessitated by LO's relationship with the SAP, the solidaristic wage policy made it imperative that all wage negotiations be coordinated by LO: only if industry-wide wage rates were bargained at the national level by LO and SAF could they remain solidaristic. This is indeed what happened. Although local unions retained some ability to bargain out wage agreements with firm-level management, they were greatly constrained by the agreements reached between LO and SAF. While centralization proved problematic by the late 1960s, during the 1950s and 1960s this centralization of authority facilitated the successful functioning of the solidaristic wage policy and thus contributed to the success of the Rehn-Meidner model.

Rehn-Meidner's success also depended on the acceptance by LO and the SAP of production oriented goals.[15] One of the three primary purposes for the Rehn-Meidner model was the rationalization and

restructuring of Swedish industry in order to increase the productive level of the Swedish economy. Although the government intervened to ensure that the burdens of economic restructuring did not fall entirely on labor in the form of unemployment, the process of restructuring, along with the technological and work organization changes it entailed, was accepted. The implications of the restructuring process, especially on the level of the shop floor, were not addressed by Social Democratic policy at the time. According to Martin:

> In other words, it was believed that government and union actions in shaping the economic conditions under which technological change took place would assure that its social consequences would be acceptable. Given these assumptions, it was accepted that decisions about technological change itself could be left up to management, compelled by competition to seek the most efficient ways of carrying out production. *Hence, there was no reason to challenge management's claim to decide unilaterally on the adoption of new technology and on the organization of work required to utilize it.*[16]

Left to themselves to determine the organization of the production process, Swedish management instituted work organizations which led to protest from the work force. The exclusively macroorientation of the Rehn-Meidner model, concerned as it was with production, employment, and price levels, failed to identify the workplace as an area of Social Democratic policy concern.[17]

2. THE CHALLENGE TO THE REHN-MEIDNER MODEL

By the mid-1960s a shift in policy orientation began to take shape, and by the early 1970s LO and the SAP had departed from this restricted focus on macro-issues of economic growth, employment, and inflation, and had adopted a concern for the micro-issues of shop-floor relations and work organization. This shift was the result of challenges posed to the union, the state, and management in the 1960s and 1970s.

The Challenge to The Union

The primary challenge to LO came from rank-and-file membership. As noted, the Rehn-Meidner model was designed to protect those workers displaced from non-competitive sectors from long-term unemployment. It did so through active labor-market policies, and through ensuring an expanding competitive sector to absorb these workers. The Rehn-Meidner model, however, did not address the problems of workers who remained employed. This policy orientation remained feasible through the 1950s and 1960s because of work-force acquiescence to rationalizations and Fordist-type work systems. By the mid-1960s, however, LO was forced to recognize that this policy had caused problems for those workers who had employment, and that the task of the labor movement could not be simply providing jobs for those displaced by structural adjustment: active labor market policies were not enough of a solution to the problems posed by this adjustment.

The rationalization of industry took a toll on the work force in various ways. This is attested to in most of the literature on this period of Swedish political economy. By the mid to late 1960s rationalizations were forcing LO rank-and-file membership to focus more on the workplace and less on the broader political economy. By largely ignoring workplace issues throughout the Fordist years, LO and the SAP thereby forced the workplace to become an issue by the late 1960s:

> In both declining and advanced sectors, the drive to raise productivity through speed-ups and work reorganization may have brought a deterioration of working conditions. In any case, management initiatives served to focus rank-and-file concerns on workplace issues, and gave rise to new demands of a 'qualitative' character.[18]

According to Stephens, because the policy focus of LO-SAP had left the course of work changes and rationalizations up to market forces, a "dehumanization of work life" was allowed to occur.[19] The LO-SAP policies of the 1950s and 1960s are also said to have produced a widespread dissatisfaction with the working environment. Elvander, for example, argues that employees were subjected to a "trying working environment,"[20] while Heclo and Madsen point out that another element of concern among Swedish workers was the structure of

authority at the workplace.[21] Faced with this combination of conditions, the work force in the late 1960s began to dissent from LO policy, and began to demand a focus on shop-floor concerns.

Conditions on the shop floor were not the only source of rank-and-file opposition to the centralized union, however. By the mid-1960s, LO also began having trouble maintaining the solidaristic wage policy. As I noted above, the setting of appropriate wage rates was difficult. If wage rates were set too low, profitable firms would be able to offer higher wages in the decentralized element of wage bargaining that did remain in place. With this "wage drift," of course, wages cease to be solidaristic and thus this element of the Rehn-Meidner model becomes dysfunctional. Additionally, wage drift tends to hinder solidarity between unions and thus to undermine the cohesion of confederal unionism and centralized bargaining. If, on the other hand, wage rates were set too high, profitable firms would not have the requisite capital for expansion, and thus this element of the Rehn-Meidner model would become dysfunctional, posing a threat to full-employment.

The ability of LO to carry out the solidaristic wage policy further depended on the SAP successfully putting pressure on corporate profits "from above." That is, the profit squeeze designed to rationalize industry was more of a profit pinch with wage pressure from below and tax pressure from above. If the SAP failed to institute sufficiently restrictive fiscal policies, the wage rate set by LO would be too low and would allow for wage drift in the most profitable firms. This is exactly what happened in the mid-1960s and in the wage round of 1969-1970. In both cases, the government failed to institute an appropriately restrictive fiscal policy and, therefore, the wage rate set by LO was far too low. During the mid-1960s wage drift exceeded contractual wage gains by 75% and in 1969-70 wage drift accounted for twice the gains brought by contractual increases. Above all else, this indicated that "LO had clearly captured a much lower portion of what it proved possible for employers to pay."[22]

As a result of LO's failure to carry out a successful solidaristic wage policy in the mid and late 1960s, the union confederation became susceptible to rank-and-file charges that it was failing to adequately defend the interests of the membership. As wage drift accounted for a greater and greater percentage of total wage gains, moreover, the solidaristic wage policy lost its credibility as a justification for centralized wage negotiations. Both of these consequences implied a threat to the centralized authority of LO. Rank-and-file dissent mounted and two unions left LO in the mid-1960s, attempting to engage only in local wage bargaining. LO's immediate response was to seek higher

wage rates that left less room for wage drift in subsequent wage rounds, but this strategy failed to solve the crisis of authority.

The combination of protest against the organization of the workplace and LO's failure to secure adequate wage agreements led to the eruption of wildcat strikes across Sweden by late 1969 and 1970. The most famous of these, the Kiruna mine strike, began in December, 1969, and during the next year over 200 unofficial strikes were recorded. There is, of course, no clearer an expression of rank-and-file dissent from centralized union authority than the wildcat strike. The wildcat strike wave of 1969-70 indicated that LO had to change its policies if it was to remain the legitimate organizational representative of the Swedish working class. The strike wave also served as a specific expression of protest against the nature of industrial work, and the authority structures which defined it. Summarizing these elements, Rianne Mahon wrote, "Like their counterparts in other Western European countries, these strikes can be interpreted as a revolt against Fordist relations of production."[23]

Through the strike wave, the Swedish working class forced LO to face a crisis of authority and to address a series of problems: the loyalty of the rank-and-file membership, a failing solidaristic wage policy, and the problematic nature of industrial work. To anticipate the next section, in order to bolster support of the membership, LO decided that increased union influence on the shop floor was crucial. Since the early postwar years, local unions' ability to engage in local wage negotiations and control the strike weapon was severely restricted, as noted above. Extending control over wage negotiations to local unions was not feasible, however, as this would have meant the end of the solidaristic wage policy and coordinated LO-SAP economic policy. Because power over wage bargaining could not be granted to the local unions, but LO's survival depended on extending local union power, the affiliate unions had to be given control over *non-wage issues.*

The problem with this approach was quite clear—§32 of SAF's constitution forbid union involvement in decisions regarding the organization of work. LO was thus forced, by the early 1970s, to challenge §32 and, thereby, to challenge the heart of the Swedish historical compromise. It was supposed, moreover, that local union influence in non-wage organization issues would not only increase member loyalty, but that it would also serve as the vehicle through which the changes in the organization of work demanded by the work force could be secured. In LO's eyes, that is, industrial democracy was the answer to all of the challenges posed in the late 1960s.

The Challenge to the Government

The SAP was also implicated in the policy focus on macro-issues, although protest against this orientation was directed mainly at LO. The main challenge to the SAP in the 1960s came in the electoral arena as a result of the rapid reconfiguration of the working class, upon which the SAP depended for electoral support. Across the 1930s, 1940s, and 1950s, this support was largely secured through blue-collar workers, often through collective affiliation of LO union members with the party. With the rapid growth of the public sector in Sweden, however, the working class was becoming increasingly populated by white-collar workers by the 1960s, and by the 1970s, the number of salaried employees was equal to one half the total number of workers in Sweden.[24] The growth of the white-collar sector was reflected in the rapid growth of the white-collar unions, especially the Central Organization of Salaried Employees (*Tjänstemännens Centralorganisation*, or TCO). Membership in the white collar unions grew by 250% between 1950 and 1970 while LO membership lists expanded by only 14%. As a result, the white-collar unions share of total union membership rose from one-fifth of the total to one-third. In 1970, TCO membership accounted for 27% of the organized work force.[25]

While LO had historically provided the SAP with its mass of support, and union membership often implied collective affiliation with the party, the same did not hold true for TCO. Although many TCO members voted for the SAP, TCO was not officially affiliated with the party and white-collar support for the SAP was certainly not guaranteed. As a result of the growth of the white-collar sector and the high rate of organization of white-collar workers within TCO, therefore, the SAP's continued electoral success came to depend on securing the votes of at least a proportion of white-collar workers. Developing a policy which both LO and TCO would support was perhaps the best way for the SAP to secure this continued success.

While blue-collar rank-and-file members were demanding qualitative changes in the nature of industrial work, and LO was beginning to favor industrial democracy as the means to achieve these changes, TCO also began to support the idea of industrial democracy. TCO had a variety of reasons for supporting this LO agenda. Primarily, joining the campaign for industrial democracy gave TCO the opportunity to represent all white-collar unions in a collective struggle, and to therein strengthen its position as a legitimate confederal authority. Moreover, the goals of industrial democracy fit well the desires of the white-collar work force

which had traditionally been apathetic about income equalization programs and hostile to policies requiring high marginal taxes, but supportive of expanded worker influence in the workplace.[26]

In the local elections of 1966, the SAP's share of the vote fell to 42.2%, the lowest since 1934, and the party lost control of Sweden's two biggest cities. Looking ahead to the next national election, the SAP, like LO at the time, was faced with a challenge to its survival. In this context, LO-TCO cooperation around the movement for industrial democracy gave the SAP enough incentive to take up the cause, and the SAP, like LO, was forced to change its policy focus. Active labor market policies and redistributive economic policies no longer sufficed to secure adequate electoral support from the working class, and a policy focus on the shop floor was needed. By the start of the 1970s the SAP had thus joined the ranks of LO (and TCO) in the drive for industrial democracy.

The Challenge to Management

While the challenge to LO came most directly in the form of wildcat strikes, and the challenge to the government came in the form of shifting electoral constituencies, the challenge to management in the 1960s came primarily in the form of high labor turnover, high rates of absenteeism, and difficulty in recruiting new workers for industrial work. Because of the tight Swedish labor market, secured through the full-employment policies of the LO-SAP coalition, these problems were made especially acute. Conditions of full-employment not only induce high rates of absenteeism and turnover, but also make it impossible for management to deal with these issues by turning to a reserve supply of labor made acquiescent by experiences of unemployment. Turnover and absenteeism problems hit Volvo especially hard. Volvo's top executive, Per Gyllenhammar commented on the effects of this by saying that "the company has to bear the costs of recruiting and training employees. The absenteeism and turnover rates also increase the costs for quality control...and for adjustments, tools and machinery."[27] For management, that is, absenteeism and turnover implied problems for profit levels which had to be addressed.

Another problem for management was that a decreasing number of people were willing to work in industry. By the mid and late 1960s education rates in Sweden had risen to the point where those typically destined for manufacturing jobs were now highly educated, and were therefore reluctant to accept factory work.[28] The younger generation of Swedes, moreover, had never experienced unemployment, or even an

economy where unemployment was a concern for the working class and, therefore, they had less tolerance for the boring and dangerous jobs offered by Swedish industry in general, and by the auto firms in particular. Finally, the provision of welfare benefits by the state made Swedish workers less dependent on wages earned at work.

While absenteeism, turnover, and recruitment difficulties would pose a challenge to management anywhere, the solidaristic wage policy made this situation especially difficult for Swedish management. That is, in order to lower rates of absenteeism and turnover, or to recruit more workers, the easiest response for management would have been offering higher wages. As I argued in Chapter One, the Fordist compromise involved acceptance of dehumanizing work environments in exchange for high wages. But in Sweden, management was unable to compensate for these conditions with higher wages due to the solidaristic wage policy. Thus, for example, Volvo could not reduce high turnover rates by raising the salary it paid to its production line workers. The alternative way to solve the problems of absenteeism, turnover, and recruitment chosen by Swedish management was experimentation with new forms of work organization. With this in mind, Pontusson wrote, "In a sense, then, work humanization can be seen as a functional equivalent of wage drift."[29]

Further, the wildcats of 1969-70 posed a challenge not only to LO, but to management as well. While to LO the strikes represented a crisis of authority, to Swedish management the strikes implied a break in the period of labor peace that had defined the Swedish economy throughout the postwar years. Indeed, from management's perspective this labor peace was a core component of Fordist stability, and without such stability production and profits were seriously threatened. In order to restore industrial peace, management was thus also forced to respond to the wildcat strike wave. Consummate with their response to the challenges of turnover, absenteeism, and recruitment difficulties, management responded to the labor unrest with experiments in new forms of work organization. With the SAP and LO committed to industrial democracy, and SAF committed to experimenting with new forms of work organization, the scene was set for addressing the challenges of the late 1960s.

3. RESPONSES TO THE CHALLENGES OF THE LATE 1960s

There were then, two trends leading towards the development of work changes in Sweden by the early 1970s. One of these was the experiments in work reorganization being carried out by SAF in response to problematic labor market conditions. In Chapter Three I argued that management-initiated work reforms in Japan were labor exclusive. Although reforms initiated and carried out by management, even if ostensibly for the benefit of employees, are prone to incorporate only managerial concerns, the Swedish case still marks a divergence from the Japanese case because Swedish management was forced to carry out these experimental changes in response to a strong labor movement. The extent to which this forced more labor inclusive and labor empowering changes will be discussed in Chapter Six.

The LO-TCO-SAP drive for industrial democracy was the second trend leading towards the development of work changes in Sweden. The industrial-democracy movement was both inspired by dissatisfaction with current work organization and designed to facilitate a union-led reorganization of work. This trend towards work reorganization thus marks the clearest break with the Japanese case, for not only were work organization changes forced by the strength of labor, but in the later stages of work reorganization labor was to have a say in the design of the new organizations themselves.

Management's Response

Before the enactment of any laws regarding industrial democracy, SAF began "socio-technical" experiments supposedly intended to build "work satisfaction" into the design of industrial work. Primarily carried out at Volvo and Saab, management believed that such work changes would solve the problems posed to them by the challenges outlined above, while also building a productivity stimulus into the work process.[30] These work experiments were intended only to change the socio-technical design of work, however, and not to lead to any changes in the authority structure within the firm. During 1968, 1969 and into 1970, LO regarded such changes as positive, and until 1970, an SAF-LO-TCO Development Council was involved in the propagation of experiments involving the breaking up of linear production processes into "flexible production system with autonomous or semi-autonomous work teams."[31]

While apparently incorporating "humanizing" elements into these work experiments, management's rationale was not simply a desire to make work better. If absenteeism, turnover, and recruitment problems were to be solved by changes in the organization of work, these work changes had to genuinely improve the quality of work life. If they did not, the challenges posed in the late 1960s would remain unsolved. Management's interest in promoting these socio-technical work experiments, however, went beyond improving work. Primarily, management was interested in offering improved working conditions as a way to pre-empt an attack on the prerogatives heretofore protected by §32. According to Higgins, SAF initiated work changes were not designed to empower workers nor to shift the fundamental balance of power within the workplace, but "on the contrary to defuse the essentially anti-social demands of employees [regarding control of the work process]—a happy conclusion for the defenders of paragraph 32!"[32]

According to Martin, management had to respond to the challenges of the late 1960s and to the new movement for industrial democracy in order to "contain and channel" the union movement, "lest it undermine management's ability to manage."[33] By improving to some extent the experience of work, that is, management hoped to avoid a labor drive for control of the production process and over the organization of work. The work changes that management initiated thus failed to upset the traditional power relations within the firm and failed to change the content of §32.

This argument, however, does not posit that the work changes weren't inspired by union pressure, nor that they didn't lead to some improvement in the quality of working life. The contrast to the Japanese situation should be clear. While Swedish management retained the initiative in these work changes, they were forced to take this initiative because of conditions in the Swedish labor market. These conditions, such as high labor turnover, high rates of absenteeism, and recruitment problems, in turn, were present because of the Social Democratic Party's commitment to full-employment, itself a reflection of labor strength. Moreover, the inability of management to solve these challenges through raising wages was the result of the institution of wage solidarity, another reflection of labor strength. Although not the direct initiator of these work experiments, the unions ability to determine the "external environment of the firm" forced management to initiate them.[34]

The Union and the Government Respond

While the first trend in the evolution of work changes was led by management, this was not the case with the movement for industrial democracy. The 1971 LO Congress adopted a policy statement on "Industrial Democracy" which demanded joint determination of issues concerning employees in the workplace. Power at the national level no longer sufficient to ensure member loyalty nor protect member interests, LO was now demanding union power on the shop floor. Because control over wage issues was not something that the centralized LO leadership was willing to relinquish, LO decided to work towards local union control over non-wage issues in order to bolster member loyalty. This implied challenging §32.

As a result, the 1971 LO Congress changed its approach to cooperating with management on socio-technical work experiments. In order to meet their objectives of increasing union control on the shop floor, LO could not continue to leave traditional workplace power relations intact. Real control and self-determination, and a voice in decision making on all issues which affected employees were called for. Ultimately, therefore, the unions had to secure influence in the planning and design of the work process. To reach these goals, LO began a drive to void §32.

Management, however, was unwilling to compromise on their fundamental prerogative to manage the firm, viewing the unions' demands for industrial democracy as "going to the root of the capitalist organization of the economy and thus to be resisted at all costs and without compromise."[35] Negotiation was therefore not a viable course of action for the unions, and in contradiction to the terms of the historical compromise, the state was brought into the labor market and legislation used to overturn §32. For the reasons outlined above, the SAP was more than willing to pass industrial democracy legislation.

Briefly, several important laws were passed between 1972 and 1977 which either directly imposed codetermination rights or strengthened the unions position within the firm.[36] Laws regarding representation of employees on the boards of corporations were passed in 1972 and 1974 which required executive boards of private companies to include two union representatives. The Security of Employment Act and Promotion of Employment Act were passed in 1974 and greatly constrained employers' rights to fire employees, while the Worker's Protection Act greatly strengthened the power of the union safety steward, giving him/her power to stop production if s/he believed a process was posing a threat to employee health or safety. In

conjunction, these laws altered the structure of authority within the firm.[37]

In terms of the movement for industrial democracy, however, the most important law was the 1977 Codetermination Act (*Medbestämmandelagen*, or MBL) which replaced earlier laws on mediation, collective bargaining, and the right of association. Most importantly, the law establishes that unions have the right to negotiate codetermination agreements with management on all matters concerning hiring and firing, work organization, and management of the production process. This nullified §32 of the SAF constitution. Indeed, to emphasize this fact, the extension of bargaining rights to these areas is contained in §32 of the new law.[38] With the passage of MBL, the stage was thus set not only for unions to demand work redesign, but to demand a voice in the redesign of the work process.

MBL, however, was only a "frame law," in that it gave unions the right to demand codetermination agreements but left it to individual unions and employers to develop these agreements. Due to employer reticence, these agreements were typically not finalized until several years after the passage of MBL. At Volvo, the codetermination agreement was not signed until 1983, and therefore it was not until the mid-1980s that the unions gained influence in the actual design of the new work organizations.

4. CONCLUSION

By way of conclusion, I should add a brief note reiterating the pressures that shaped the actual form that work changes took in the Swedish auto industry. Most important, and in contrast to the Japanese case, the Swedish work reforms took place within the context of the crisis of Fordism and, as such, the pressures for redesign of work discussed in Chapter Two were brought to bear on the Swedish auto industry. The need to respond to unstable international markets which increasingly demanded a variated product mix forced the Swedish auto makers to develop a flexible production system, and thus a flexible organization of work. Sweden was, moreover, especially vulnerable to the crisis of Fordism and the demands of the international market due to the openness of its economy and its heavy dependence on foreign trade.[39] Additionally, like the Japanese producers in the early 1950s, the Swedish makers had very small productive capacities. Again, the combination of low productive capacity and the need for product

variation called for flexible work organization.[40] A more thorough explanation of these pressures was presented above, and I will not rehash the discussion here.

The shape of the work changes in Swedish auto was not, however, determined only by these market imperatives, as this chapter shows. While the post-Fordist economy demanded flexibility, as the Japanese economy of the 1950s had, the type of flexibility developed was influenced by labor strength. Through shaping the Swedish economy, Swedish unions were able to constrain managements' choices such that work changes which allowed flexibility of production also had a positive impact on working life. Later, with the implementation of MBL codetermination rights, the unions were able to demand that work reorganization led not only to flexibility but also to a redesign of the nature of automobile work and a realignment of the authority structure within the automobile plant.

NOTES

1. Walter Korpi, *The Working Class in Welfare Capitalism: Work, Unions and Politics in Sweden* (Boston: Routledge and Kegan Paul, 1978), p. 64.

2. Korpi, p. 335.

3. Charting the course for this Social Democratic movement in the early 20th Century, Per Albin Hansson cited three successive goals: political democracy, social democracy, and economic democracy. (Winton Higgins, "Industrial Democracy and the Control Issue in Sweden," in Ed Davis and Russell Lansbury, *Democracy and Control in the Workplace* (Australia: Longman Cheshire, 1986), p. 251.) Yet, while the goals of the party were revolutionary, the SAP always advocated reformist means by which to attain these goals: it was through the participation of the working class in the political process that society was to be transformed.

4. Andrew Martin, "Trade Unions in Sweden: Strategic Responses to Change and Crisis," in Peter Gourevitch, Andre Martin, George Ross, et al. *Unions and Economic Crisis: Britain, West Germany and Sweden* (Boston: George Allen and Unwin, 1984), p. 196.

5. Lennart Forsebäck *Industrial Relations and Employment in Sweden* (Uppsala: The Swedish Institute, 1980), pp. 8-9.

6. Hugh Heclo and Henrik Madsen, *Policy and Politics in Sweden: Principled Pragmatism* (Philadelphia: Temple University Press, 1987), p. 112.

7. Korpi, p. 80; Martin, 1984, p. 193.

8. Martin (1984). p. 201.

9. N. Elvander, "Sweden," in Benjamin C Roberts, ed., *Towards Industrial Democracy* (Montclair: Allanheld, Osmun Publishers, 1979), p. 145.

10. Elvander, p. 145.

11. Korpi, p. 83.

12. Korpi, p. 87.

13. Inflation was also especially costly to Sweden, as Sweden was highly dependent on export markets. See Wolfgang Streeck, "Industrial Relations and Industrial Change: the Restructuring of the World Automobile Industry in the 1970s and 1980s," *Economic and Industrial Democracy* Vol. 8 (1987), pp. 439-441.

14. Matin (1984), p. 205.

15. By "production" oriented goals I refer to, contrary to Stephen's terminology, the LO-SAP focus on economy wide productivity, as well as on macro-issues of economic growth such as employment levels and inflation. In contrast to production issues, I discuss issues relating to the shop floor below.

16. Andrew Martin, "Sweden: Industrial Democracy and Social Democratic Strategy," in G David Garson, ed., *Worker Self Management in Industry: The West European Experience* (New York: Praeger Publishers, 1977), p. 64. My emphasis.

17. Although my discussion here focuses on those elements of the Swedish political economy which eventually impacted the development of new forms of work organization, I would note one additional component of the Rehn-Meidner model. As I argued in Chapter One, the Fordist model of wage bargaining depends on international stability. This was especially true for Sweden because, even during the Fordist years, its economy was open to international competition, and was indeed highly dependent on international trade (See below. Also see Peter J Katzenstein, *Small States in World Markets: Industrial Policy in Europe* (Ithaca: Cornell University Press, 1985). Because of this, the ability of LO and SAF to bargain appropriate wages depended on their ability to predict the future of international markets. Thus besides the successful functioning of the SAP's fiscal and labor market policies, and LO's wage policy of solidarity, the success of the Rehn-Meidner model depended on the stability of international markets.

18. Jonas Pontusson, "Radicalism and Retreat in Swedish Social Democracy," *The New Left Review* Number 165 (Sept/Oct 1987), p. 16.

19. John D Stephens, *The Transition from Capitalism to Socialism* (Urbana and Chicago: University of Illinois Press, 1979), p. 183.

20. Elvander, p. 147.

21. Heclo and Madsen, p. 121.

22. Martin (1984), p. 237.

23. Mahon, p. 303. As noted in Chapter One, the opposition to the Fordist organization of work, expressed by labor union militancy, is a component of the crisis of Fordism.

24. Korpi, p. 313.

25. Martin (1984), p. 238.

26. Stephens, p. 182. From another perspective, the growth of the white-collar sector, and more particularly the unionization of these white-collar workers, made an attack on capital—which the movement for industrial democracy quite surely was—more feasible. As Korpi put it, the history of white-collar unionization can be seen as analogous to the severing of the "ties binding the salaried employees to their employers." (p. 65) By 1970, approximately 70% of the Swedish work force was affiliated with either LO or TCO, and thus 70% of the work force constituted a "wage-earners front" willing to challenge capital and managerial prerogatives over the design of work.

27. Jonas Pontusson, "The Politics of New Technology and Job Redesign: A Comparison of Volvo and British Leyland," *Economic and Industrial Democracy* Vol 11 (1990), p. 328.

28. See, for example, Lynda King Taylor, "Worker Participation in Sweden," *Industrial and Commercial Training* (1973), p. 8.

29. Pontusson (1990), p. 328.

30. Elvander, p. 150.

31. Higgins, p. 254. Discussion of these work changes will come in Chapter Six.

32. Higgins, p. 253.

33. Martin (1977), p. 68.

34. Pontusson (1990), pp. 313-314.

35. Higgins, p. 258.

36. The slew of legislation that passed through the Riksdag in the 1970s is very familiar, and summaries of it exist in almost all of the literature on this period. See, for example Elvander, pp. 147-149. Also

see Sten Edlund and Birgitta Nyström, *Developments in Swedish Labor Law* (Stockholm: The Swedish Institute, 1988).

    37. Elvander, p. 147-148; Martin (1977), p. 49.

    38. Elvander, p. 148; Martin (1977), p. 50.

    39. See, for example, Katzenstein.

    40. Berggren, p. 57.

Chapter Five
The Toyota Model of Work Organization

By way of introducing this chapter I would like to point out a difficulty inherent in writing about a "model of work organization." First, an organization of work is a coherent system which operates as one entity: for the designers of the system, as well as for those who experience it directly, a work organization is not a conjunction of distinct components. It is not only quite difficult but also risky, therefore, to disaggregate a system into component parts. Unfortunately, such a disaggregation seems the only way to present clearly this system of work organization. Thus, while in this chapter I discuss the Toyota shop floor as if it were made up of several separate components, in actuality all of the elements discussed below are part of one unified work organization.

Further, the literature available on work organization in the Japanese auto industry is surprisingly scant. An enormous amount has been written on the Japanese "management system," but this literature focuses on such things as lifetime employment and "cooperative" labor-management relations, neglecting the actual organization of the shop floor. While these elements of the "management system" are clearly central to the study of the Japanese firm, the Japanese political economy, and the study of Japanese industrial and labor relations, they do not constitute a study of work organization. The literature that does exist on the actual organization of work within the Japanese auto firm, moreover, is predominantly written by and for industrial management and, as such, tends to be uncritical and largely non-analytic. The critical accounts that do exist are primarily written about Japanese auto "transplants" in the United States and Europe.

I have chosen the Toyota Motor Company as my case study for Japan for several reasons. Primarily, both case studies presented in this book represent the most evolved examples of work reorganization—the "highest cases"—which reflect the greatest changes in the organization of work. Toyota, under the leadership of Ohno Taiichi, engaged in more extensive work organization innovations than any of the other auto

makers, and thus it is Toyota that best represents the Japanese "model" of work organization.

Because I have chosen Toyota, it is important to understand, as I stressed in Chapter Three, why a case study of Toyota is appropriate following a discussion of the Nissan strike of 1953. As noted, the Nissan strike not only represented the crushing of the Nissan company union but was also the signal event in the defeat of the independent industrial union movement in Japan, ensuring the dominance of ineffectual enterprise unions across the auto industry. As a result, management at Toyota, as well as at Nissan, was given a free hand to implement the form of work organization that best met their needs.

1. FLEXIBLE PRODUCTIVITY

The overriding goal of the Toyota system of work organization is ensuring high levels of productivity, and flexibility in the production process and in the products manufactured. This flexibility is secured through the development of a flexible work force and a flexible production system.

A Functionally Flexible Work Force

The flexibility of the Toyota work force underlies the entire Toyota production system, and is central to ensuring that the firm can manufacture a variated product mix, and that it can respond quickly and efficiently to changes in demand. Such responses are primarily achieved through labor mobility within the firm, and in order to facilitate this labor force redeployment, all workers are required to perform a variety of tasks, at a variety of work stations, using a variety of machines.[1]

The organization of Toyota workers into groups—or teams—responsible for a certain segment of the production line is the first element in this work-force flexibility. Once the work force is organized into teams, management has the discretion to reallocate team members to new tasks according to the needs of the market, without opposition from the unions or workers.[2] When demand varies or market composition changes, Toyota management has the ability to change job assignments, to order workers to work a greater or lesser number of machines, to perform the same tasks at different cycle times, etc. The details of these changes will be discussed below, but here it is

important to note the role that managerial authority has in securing labor flexibility. This is in clear contrast to the situation in American auto firms, for example, where strong union enforcement of job rules and classifications would prevent management from making such unilateral changes.

The advantages of work-force flexibility for management are clear. Primarily, with a flexible work force, a variated product mix can be manufactured and changes in the level and constitution of demand dealt with through labor mobility within the firm. A flexible work force, moreover, alleviates the effects of absenteeism because if one team member is absent, management is able to reorganize work in such a way that the remaining workers compensate for their absent teammate. While there are advantages of flexibility for management, there are also potential costs. Primarily, in order for workers to be easily transferred form one job to another they must be able to perform several jobs adequately, and to operate all the machines employed in each of the jobs to which they may be reassigned. This presents the threat of high training costs. To avoid such costs, while ensuring that workers are able to do almost any task within the factory, jobs are designed to have as little skill content as possible. As Parker and Slaughter put it, "The less training and skill required, the greater the interchangeability without increasing costs. Multiskilling every worker means deskilling every job."[3] The process by which jobs are deskilled and made easily transferable, and the work force made flexible, is quite reminiscent of Taylorist standardization of tasks.

Besides facilitating the easy transfer of tasks and thus flexibility, standardization of tasks fills another of the needs expressed by Japanese management. One problem with the traditional Fordist assembly line was the difficulty managers had with "line balancing"—the process by which tasks are divided among workers in such a way that the line flows at a constant rate, while ensuring that all workers are actively engaged in work at all times. If, for example, one worker's task takes only 30 seconds while the majority of other workers need 60 seconds to complete their tasks, this worker will be idle 30 seconds out of every minute and the line will be unbalanced. In order to achieve a balanced line, cycle times—the time spent completing one complete task—for all workers must therefore be the same.

Even when cycle times are the same for all workers, however, if assembly tasks require any skill, differentials in skill levels between workers will result in some workers finishing their tasks before others. This implies that some workers will have "idle time," and again, the line will be unbalanced. In order to prevent such unbalance, tasks at

Toyota are rigidly standardized and all workers required to follow strictly the standardized steps laid out by management. In this way, management ensures that all tasks involve no skills, all tasks take exactly the same time, and all "idle time" is avoided. This standardization and balancing process also ensures that all workers are actively employed as close to 60 seconds out of every minute as possible.[4]

Two steps are involved in the process of standardizing work at Toyota: the establishment of the cycle time and the creation of a standard operations routine. In both cases, management dictates the speed and content of work. Because all workers must have tasks which have the same cycle time in order to balance the assembly line, it is necessary to establish a standard cycle time. The length of the cycle has, of course, critical implications for the labor force. First, as cycle times get shorter, the proportion of the final product contributed by each worker gets smaller. Such fragmentation of work has the effect of denying workers a sense of connection with the production of a complete product, an element of the Marxist conception of alienation. As Kamata put it, "Even if the work had wider variety and the production speed was left to the workers, the work was still fragmentary, *lacking any sense of creation.*"[5] Second, if cycle times decrease but the amount of work required within each cycle doesn't change, workers have to work faster. If one person is responsible for assembling a gear box and the cycle time is two minutes, this worker has two minutes in which to build his/her gear box. If, however, the cycle time is one minute, the same gear box must be built in a minute less time.

While management is forced to recognize a certain physical limit on the pace of work, the determination of the cycle time at Toyota does not take into account the effects of work speed on the work force. Rather, the cycle time is determined by dividing the required daily quantity of output into the effective daily operating time. In other words, management determines how many units must be produced in one day, and divides this into the amount of working time available each day, and the result is the cycle time! The effect of cycle time and work speed on the work force is clearly not considered in this equation. Moreover, the effective daily operating time is not reduced to take account for machine problems, idle time spent waiting for materials, rework, the effects of fatigue, or work breaks. Consequently, the cycle time is calculated assuming that workers are working every second of every day even though, due to the list of factors just noted, this is not

the case. As a result, cycle times are even lower and the work pace even faster.[6]

Once the standard cycle time is established, the next step in the standardization of work is the determination of the standard operations routine, which dictates the process by which every segment of every task is to be carried out, and the dissemination of standard operations routine sheets to the work force. These operations sheets are so detailed that instructions for tasks taking as little as one second are spelled out. That is, every motion a worker takes, including moving from one task or machine to another, picking up and using tools, etc., is prescribed by management through these work sheets. The standard operations routine work sheets are posted at each work station to ensure that workers are aware of exactly how they are to perform their tasks. Indeed, it is one of the supervisor's primary responsibilities to make sure that all work is done according to the work sheets.[7]

While management gains a flexible work force through this type of multi-tasking, the implications of this standardization for workers are severe. In an environment of rigidly prescribed work routines, the autonomy of the work force is severely restricted, if not completely eliminated. Workers are not able to determine for themselves how best to carry out the tasks they are assigned, precluding a creative engagement with the work process and preventing workers from changing the way they do their work in order to relieve over-stressed muscles. While first-hand accounts of work life in Toyota plants in Japan, in English, are rare, Satoshi Kamata's *Japan in the Passing Lane* provides us with some insights into the effects of the standardization of work on the work force. Kamata worked on the assembly line at Toyota in Japan and reports the following:

> Here at Toyota 'to learn' means merely to acquire the ability to keep up with the line, quickly repeating certain physical movements while thinking absolutely nothing . . . Each individual worker has his own way of working and should be entitled to produce goods in his own way. There should be a variety of working methods. But in fact, there is only one method of producing goods in the fastest possible way: standardized work . . . Under such a system, all our movements must become mechanical and habitual. Only if we stop thinking and unconsciously follow this system can we keep up. Our bodies are treated as if they were machines.[8]

This observation is especially important in light of the claims that the Toyota system provides workers an opportunity to expand their skills and is a step towards the improvement and rehumanization of work. The Toyota system does indeed incorporate job rotation and multi-machining into the production process, and many see this as an improvement over the Fordist system of work organization, where each worker performs only one task at one machine.[9] As a result of job rotation and responsibility for operating multiple machine, the claim is made that Toyota workers are not only flexible but they are "multi-skilled." As Monden claims with regard to job rotation at Toyota:

> The various benefits can best be summarized with the simple words: respect for humans. This is a considerably different attitude from traditional schemes where mass production yields a division of labor and, in turn, specialization of labor, simplification of jobs, and, finally, human alienation.[10]

Implicit in his claim is that work at Toyota is neither specialized nor simplified, and workers are therefore not alienated.

The difference between "multi-skilling" and "multi-tasking" explains the discrepancy between Kamata's description of work at Toyota and the boasts of many in management circles that the Toyota system is a rehumanized system. By understanding the extent to which tasks are standardized at Toyota, we are able to understand the actual nature of "multi-skilled work" at Toyota. As explained in the discussion on line balancing, not only are workers not required to have multiple skills at Toyota, they are in fact prevented from having any skills at all. In order to perform the various tasks inherent in job rotation, Toyota workers, in Parker and Slaughter's terms, must only have dexterity, stamina, and the ability to follow instructions. No skills which require training or specialized knowledge are needed. While one task may be slightly different from another, or one machine slightly different from another, when Toyota workers rotate between different tasks or different machines, only different variations of similar repetitive tasks are called for. Rather than requiring "multi-skilling," the system at Toyota simply requires workers to be able to carry out multiple unskilled tasks. In Kamata's words:

Only three people, the foreman, the team chief, and
the subchief are able to handle each work process of
the transmission assembly. But in reality, they're
neither unskilled nor skilled—not even half-skilled.
Their jobs have nothing at all to do with skill. Like
the rest of us . . . they go through motions that are
not 'skills' in any sense of the word, just primitive
movements . . . It makes no difference whether you're
assembling engines or drive shafts. As long as you're
on the line, it's all the same.[11]

One component of job rotation at Toyota actually involves the
deskilling of work. In the drive to make the production system flexible,
set-up times at Toyota have been drastically reduced. Set-up time is the
time it takes to prepare the production system for production. Thus, for
example, the preparation of dies and presses to make car bodies and
body parts have calculated set-up times. Part of the time needed to
prepare a die or press for a new production run involves adjustment of
machinery and is, therefore, known as adjustment time. The adjustment
of dies and presses typically requires skilled labor and is not performed
by production workers but by workers who have specialized training in
this area. At Toyota, however, the need for skilled die and press
adjusters has been designed out of the system. In order to facilitate the
incorporation of die and press set-up into the job rotations of unskilled
production workers this work has been standardized, and while die and
press adjustment are part of a production worker's expanded job retinue,
this does not represent an expansion of multi-skilling. For production
workers, the standardization of die and press set-up means one more
unskilled task to perform, while for management this standardization
implies the elimination of skilled work within the factory. Again, by
"multi-skilling" every worker, every job is deskilled.

A further, and final, component of work-force flexibility is
management's ability to assign overtime freely. Some of the bitter
labor-management struggles of the early 1950s were fought over
management's right to unilaterally assign overtime, as shown in
Chapter Three, and the defeat of labor meant, among other things, that
management had won this right. While the entire system of labor
flexibility ensures that Toyota can produce a variated product line and
can respond quickly to changes in demand, in order to respond to short-
term increases in the level of demand, Toyota management assigns
overtime. Kamata's account of life at Toyota is full of references to
overtime enforced by management in response to increases in the level

of demand. Freedom to assign overtime, moreover, gives management more flexibility in determining production quotas or cycle times. If workers are unable to fill quotas by the end of the day, or can't keep up with dictated cycle times, they are simply forced to keep working until the quotas have been filled.

A Flexible Production System

Before examining Toyota's renowned Just-in-Time (JIT) work system, it is worthwhile to understand some of the elements of the production design which make the Toyota system flexible. Again, the division between these elements (low lead times, U shaped production lines, and mixed model production) and the JIT system discussed below is fairly artificial and employed only for the sake of clarity.

The first component of the flexible production system is the reduction of lead time—the time between the order for a particular product and the final assembly of that product. In order to respond rapidly to customer demands, and especially to changes in those demands, lead time must be as low as possible. A primary component in the reduction in lead time has been the establishment of rapid set-up times. When the constitution of demand changes, i.e., new models or a different mix of models are ordered, the production line has to adapt. This involves the preparation of, for example, new die and press configurations. The longer it takes to set up these dies and presses the longer it takes to adapt the production line to the new market demands, and thus the longer it takes to fill the new orders—the longer the lead time. By reducing set-up times, Toyota has been able to reduce lead times and facilitate rapid responses to changes in the demand for automobiles. Between 1959 and 1960, Toyota reduced die set-up time from 2-3 hours to only 15 minutes, and press set-up times in the 1970s were as low as three minutes.[12] In contrast, set-up times in traditional Fordist plants are several hours or longer.

Rapid set-up times facilitate another element of production flexibility—mixed model assembly. In a Fordist auto plant each production line produces only one standardized product, as discussed in Chapter One. This system works only so long as there is stable mass demand for such standardized goods, but if model variations are demanded, as in the post-Fordist economy and as has been the case in Japan since the 1950s, this Fordist model proves inflexible. Because dies, presses, etc. could be changed so rapidly, and because the labor force could adapt to these changes, Toyota was able to begin producing different car models on *the same assembly line*. Instead of producing

thousands and thousands of one model before any production of a different model could begin, Toyota is thus able to simultaneously produce all the models demanded by the market. In this way, it is in an excellent position to respond rapidly to shifts in demand.

Finally, in order to facilitate multi-machining and internal labor mobility, the actual design of production lines at Toyota was changed. Instead of one linear flow, production lines were designed as a series of U shape collections of work stations which facilitated multi-machining by allowing each worker to operate machines on both sides of the U. Further, by designing production in this way, an increase or decrease in the number of workers employed as a result of market changes was also facilitated. If demand increased enough to warrant adding more workers, the number of workers inside each U would be increased, and each worker would be responsible for fewer work stations. If demand fell, the number of workers working inside each U would decrease and each worker would be responsible for working more stations along the U.[13]

2. THE JUST-IN-TIME SYSTEM

While the flexibility of the work force and production system is crucial to the Toyota work organization, perhaps the most well known component of the Toyota system is the Just-In-Time (JIT) organization of work and production. JIT is, in the most general sense, a system of work organization in which all resources, both material and human, are minimized and constantly in use. Although JIT is widely heralded as an inventory reduction program, and while this is certainly one of its primary aims, the JIT system is a broader method for organizing workers, for transmitting information throughout the production process, for minimizing all resources (workers and materials), for adding flexibility to production, for continuously rationalizing production, and for controlling quality.

Pull Production and Kanban

The central organizing principle of JIT production is "pull production." Ohno organized work at Toyota in such a way that the demands of final assembly "pulled" production through the plant backwards from the final production process. That is, starting with final assembly, Toyota workers go back to the previous station to get the parts they need for their assembly task. In a traditional Fordist plant,

production quotas were set separately for each assembly station, and in this way assembly was "pushed" through to final assembly. At Toyota, on the other hand, quotas for finished products dictate the levels of production required from all other work stations. That production could be tailored exactly to the demands of the market is the primary advantage of pull production. Once market demand is calculated, a quota for final assembly is set, and the JIT system ensures that production at all other stages is be pulled along in due course. In order for this system to function, however, an accurate information system which can communicate production needs backwards through the production process is needed.

To meet this need, the kanban card system was developed. A kanban is a card which communicates information about production within Toyota and between Toyota and its supplier firms. Within Toyota, there are two types of kanban: a withdrawal kanban, and a production ordering kanban. The withdrawal kanban indicates the type and quantity of product which the subsequent—closer to final assembly—work station needs to withdraw from the preceding—further from final assembly—process. A production ordering kanban indicates the type and quantity of product which the preceding work station must produce, as dictated by the needs of the subsequent station.

With these two types of kanban in use, the JIT production system works as follows. Each work station has an inbound and an outbound stock point. A subsequent, or downstream, work station sends withdrawal kanbans along with empty containers to the outbound stock point of the work station immediately previous to it on the production line. This is effectively an order for parts sent from the subsequent to the preceding, or upstream, station. When the withdrawal kanbans and the empty containers arrive at the preceding station, parts produced here are placed in the empty containers and sent to the inbound stock point of the subsequent station. Each part produced by the preceding station will have had a production ordering kanban attached to it. When these parts are withdrawn and sent—"pulled"—to the subsequent station, the production ordering kanbans are removed and placed on a production ordering kanban "post," at the preceding station. Once on this post, the production ordering kanbans instruct the preceding station to produce more parts in accordance to the number of kanbans. It is thus the withdrawal of parts by the subsequent station that instructs the preceding station to produce. Newly assembled parts are then placed in the outbound stock point where they await the arrival of withdrawal kanbans from the subsequent station.[14]

Beyond establishing pull production, moreover, the use of kanbans functions in two other ways. First, the kanban system ensures that only those components needed by subsequent stations, and ultimately by final assembly, are produced, and that they are produced only when they are needed. In this sense they ensure that each part in the production process is produced only just-in-time for use by the next station. Second, the total number of kanban establishes the amount of work-in-progress inventory allowed in the system. Work-in-progress inventory are those parts which remain in the outbound stock points awaiting withdrawal by the subsequent station. The goal of JIT production is to minimize these buffer inventories by minimizing the number of kanbans. Recall that the number of components at each stock point is equal to the number of kanbans, so as this number is reduced the buffer inventories are reduced as well.[15]

Minimization of Resources and Inventoryless Production

The minimization of production resources, including materials and workers, is the second component of the JIT system. By minimizing the number of kanbans used between each pair of work stations, and by ensuring that each station produces only the parts and components ordered by the kanbans, the JIT system works to eliminate all inventories of materials. Almost as soon as a component is produced by a preceding station it is withdrawn by the subsequent station for use in further assembly. Throughout the entire production system, therefore, inventories are reduced to a bare minimum.

Inventory reduction is cost effective, as there are a whole series of costs associated with inventories, including the interest costs on the value of products held in inventory. There are also indirect costs associated with holding inventory, such as the salaries of those employed to handle material inventory, etc. Beyond such costs, however, producing inventories hinders the ability of firms to respond flexibly to changes in demand. Minimizing inventories reduces lead times, and thus enhances flexible response to customer demand.[16] In clear contrast to Fordist systems where inventories were produced "just-in-case" something went wrong in the production process, moreover, the JIT system forbids the production of any inventories and, therefore, makes the production system quite vulnerable to problems and defects. As will be discussed in detail below, this is a primary goal of the JIT system.

Besides minimizing materials inventory and removing buffers against production problems and defects, the JIT system also minimizes

the amount of available labor. Again in contrast to the just-in-case Fordist organization, no extra workers are employed at Toyota to protect against absenteeism. If a member of a production team is absent, the team leader fills in for the absent worker but no replacement for either the absent worker or the team leader is provided.

The minimization of materials and workers is not, however, a one time, static process. Rather, the JIT system achieves continuous rationalization through the continuous removal of materials and workers. At a given level of materials and workers, production is monitored by management through direct surveillance by foremen and through a visual display system known as the andon system. The andon system is a series of green, yellow, and red lights above each work station which reflect different conditions of production. If the green light is illuminated, work at a given station is running smoothly with adequate materials and an adequate number of workers. If the yellow light is illuminated, materials are in short supply and the workers are stressed to keep up with the line. A yellow light signals the team leader that assistance is needed. A red light indicates that there are not enough materials and that a worker or workers have fallen far enough behind the pace of production to warrant stopping the line. In the JIT system, the ideal is to have all stations running with yellow lights illuminated. At this level of production, inventories are as low as possible, and the number of workers is similarly minimized to the greatest possible extent.

When green lights are illuminated, however, production is running smoothly enough, in management's eyes, to allow for further rationalization.[17] In order to increase the level of productive efficiency, management can reduce the number of kanbans in order to remove more buffer stock. As buffers decline, inventory costs are reduced and the system becomes more flexible. With the reduction in buffers, workers are forced to keep pace with an even further stressed production system, and to maintain stricter and stricter quality standards because the lower the buffer level, the lower is the system's tolerance for defects. After each reduction in the number of kanbans, an adjustment period follows where production runs with yellow or even red lights illuminated. Once the work force adjusts to lower buffer levels, however, and green lights are again illuminated, another round of resource minimization occurs. This is, then, a process of continuous rationalization.[18]

When production is running at the green light pace, management may also remove workers from the production line, forcing the remaining work force to improve production speeds in order to reach the same quotas with fewer workers. Whenever Toyota workers complete

their jobs ahead of cycle time—when, in management's terms they have "idle time"—they are instructed to stand completely still for the remainder of the cycle. If, for example, cycle time is 60 seconds, and one group of workers is able to complete their task in 50 seconds, they are told to stand still for the 10 seconds they are not working. This gives a clear sign to management that rationalization is in order. If there are 10 workers in this group, according to managerial logic the group is doing only 500 seconds of work in a cycle which allows for 600 seconds of work. If one worker is removed from the group, the remaining nine are forced to do the same 500 seconds worth of work. But with only nine workers in the team, each must be actively employed for 56 seconds out of every minute. By increasing each worker's active employment by six seconds every minute, the same work gets done with one less worker. This of course, is cost effective.

Toyota management does not, however, simply wait around for workers to complete their jobs ahead of cycle times. On the contrary, Toyota management engages in a continuous attempt to minimize "wasted motions."[19] That is, through surveillance of the production system, and through employee suggestions (see below), faster ways of completing individual tasks are developed. Once wasted motions are identified, the standard operations routines are revised to eliminate these motions and lower the time necessary for each production process. In this way, a work process which took 60 seconds can be reduced to 55 seconds. However, once the necessary work time is reduced to 55 seconds, the process begins again, again more "unnecessary" motions are identified and eliminated, reducing the allotted time still further. In eight years, the allotted time for assembly of a transmission at Toyota was reduced nearly 50%, from 75 to 45 seconds, through a series of such rationalizations.[20]

The reduction of time allotted for each task through Taylorist rationalization, and the removal of workers through the elimination of idle time are, of course, linked. As the time necessary to carry out specific tasks falls, previously fully engaged workers now find themselves with idle time, and as idle time builds it becomes possible for management to remove workers from the line in order to ensure constant active engagement. The process keeps repeating. Once workers are removed, a period of adjustment follows where production lines are stressed, and line stoppages may occur. However, once the work force adjusts to the elimination of workers, and production lines again run smoothly, more wasted motions are identified and eliminated, more idle time results, and more workers are removed. The result, as noted above, is a process of continuous rationalization. In Kamata's words:

The rationalization here is not so much to eliminate work as, more directly to eliminate workers. For example, if 33% of 'wasted motion' is eliminated from three workers, one worker becomes unnecessary. The history of Toyota rationalization is a history of the reduction of workers, and that's the secret of how Toyota shows no increase in employees while achieving its startling increases in production. All free time [wasted motions/idle time] during working hours has been taken away from assembly-line workers as wasteful. All their time, to the last second is devoted to production.[21]

It is this dynamic function of JIT that is perhaps its ultimate function.

The Intensification of Work

As the number of workers available to perform the necessary labor decreases, the intensity of work required from those who remain increases in several ways. First, and most obviously, the production of a car involves a definite amount of labor and as the work force is depleted, fewer and fewer workers are available to perform this same amount of labor. As a result, each worker becomes responsible for more labor. At the same time, however, the time allotted to perform this labor *decreases*. With the continual improvement of the standard operations routines, workers are forced to perform more work in less time. If assembling a gear box previously took 60 seconds, after the elimination of wasted motions the same gear box must be assembled in less time. This of course, is a work speed-up.

Assembly times are, moreover, never long enough to allow workers anything approaching a leisurely pace. Reductions in time allotted for task completion mean going from one intense work pace to an even more intense pace. Idle time, a term coined by managerial observers, only results from workers laboring at breakneck paces which slightly outpace a "murderous" conveyor speed.[22] This is clearly attested to by Kamata's account of the rationalization of his job at Toyota. When he first started working he had well over one minute to complete his task. At this pace, he describes his experience of production work in the following ways:

> Almost as soon as I begin, I am dripping with sweat
> . . . I'm thirsty as hell, but workers can neither
> smoke nor drink water. Going to the toilet is out of
> the question . . . Once I fall behind the line pace, I'm
> unable to get back to my regular position. Though I
> double my efforts, using twice as much energy, I just
> can't recover the lost seconds. It's like I imagine hell
> to be . . . [And after a day at this pace] I'm tired. I
> don't believe anybody could be more tired. Is this
> what 'labor-intensive' means? I never imagined there
> was labor so 'intense' that you couldn't rest even one
> second.[23]

This is Kamata's experience *before* any wasted motions are removed, before any idle time is identified and eliminated, before any of his fellow workers are removed from the line and the rest of the team becomes responsible for the excess work. When the rationalizations do occur, Kamata has to perform this same task in even less time. Indeed, over the course of several years, the time allotted for Kamata's task was reduced by nearly 50%.

The minimization of materials and work-in-progress inventory also leads to an increased work intensity. In a traditional production system it is possible for workers to build up stocks of components prior to the time that these components are actually needed. By working ahead of the line, and building buffers, workers in a Fordist plant are able to secure a period of rest. Once such buffers are built, workers can rest until the buffers are depleted. Such buffer building is impossible at Toyota because, according to the minimization of resources principle, components are only to be produced when ordered by kanban. The number of kanban, in addition, is reduced to a bare minimum in order to prevent the buildup of any work-in-progress inventory, thereby preventing the building of any buffers. Even if it were possible to build buffers of material, moreover, the rest time that the workers would be able to achieve by doing so would become idle time in the eyes of management, and would subsequently be rationalized out of existence. As a result of the JIT system, it is therefore impossible for workers at Toyota to secure any break time for themselves. The pace of work described by Kamata above continues uninterrupted, except for one 45 minute break in a nine or ten hour shift.

A final factor in the process of work intensification is the contribution to this process made by the workers themselves. A much heralded component of the Toyota work organization is the supposed

involvement of the employees in the design of work. In the process of rationalizing production, input from employees, through quality circles and an individual suggestion system, is sought by management. If a Toyota worker believes there is a way to eliminate a step in the completion of his/her production work, or a way to perform any step a little faster, s/he is "encouraged" to suggest this to management. If a team of workers believes it would be possible to eliminate one worker from their team, and still complete the necessary work within the cycle time, they are to suggest this to management. However, any changes which improve the production system—for example, by reducing the amount of time needed to perform a certain task—and could serve to give workers a bit of breathing space, result rather in the reduction of resources or workers, or in the increase of work required of the workers whose jobs have been "improved." If one worker suggests a way to complete his/her task in 10 fewer seconds, s/he will be assigned ten more seconds of work to ensure that s/he is working as close to 60 seconds a minute as possible. In other words, the contribution of Toyota employees to the design of work amounts to a self-imposed speed-up.[24]

This self-imposition of work intensification is secured through a wage and promotion system in which the approval of managers is necessary for workers to receive bonuses and/or promotions. In fact, bonuses at Toyota can amount to 50% of normal monthly pay.[25] These bonuses are awarded, at the discretion of management, according to the production efficiency of individual workers and according to the worker's "attitude" towards the firm.[26] A good attitude is clearly displayed by the contribution of suggestions as to how work can be continually rationalized. Because such a large percentage of actual wages is dependent on management approval, Toyota workers have little choice but to contribute to the intensification of their own work.[27] Kamata comments on his experience of this component of the Toyota system in this way:

> When I get to the line, I notice an oil feeder with a thin plastic hose hanging overhead. The team chief tells me to oil the gears when an RK or RY transmission comes by [a task for which Kamata was not previously responsible]. Another operation! Already there's barely enough time to do the regular job . . . This must be one of the 'Good Idea Suggestions' some worker made in order to fulfill his assignment.[28]

In-Process Quality Control

While the elimination of inventories and the speed-up of production this elimination entails are certainly goals in themselves, this elimination also allows for a new system of quality control. In the Fordist work organization, quality control is performed by quality control inspectors through statistical sampling. A percentage of components and finished products—produced in large batches—is inspected for quality after it has been produced. If a batch has less than a set number of defects it passes inspection. All problems, identified by the inspectors, are corrected *after* final assembly by groups of rework specialists.

The JIT system, in contrast, builds quality control into the production process itself through the reduction of inventories.[29] With a minimal amount of work-in-progress inventory, all defects are immediately apparent and problematic. When a downstream station receives a defective part, no buffer stocks are available to substitute for the defect, making the JIT system quite vulnerable to defects. This vulnerability is, however, exactly management's intention. Because there is no way to compensate for defective parts, problems are identified at their source and must be corrected there immediately.[30] If a defective part which can't be corrected within the allotted cycle time appears anywhere in the production process, workers supposedly have "the power and the responsibility to stop the line."[31] Once production stops, the cause of the defect is sought out and eliminated at its source.

This system is much better able to ensure quality production than is a system based on quality control inspectors and statistical sampling. In the JIT system, all quality defects are caught because production cannot continue until every problem is corrected. Because this quality system reduces the need for any post-production rework and the need for employees involved only in quality inspection, it is cost effective. Yet the process which implies better quality and lower production costs for Toyota also places the responsibility for quality control on the production line workers. Workers themselves must identify and correct all mistakes in order to ensure that production runs smoothly enough to allow the elimination of all buffer stocks. While devolution of responsibility could imply a positive broadening of work content, workers are not allotted any extra time for these indirect tasks. Thus, while job content expands cycle times do not. The result is a further speed-up and intensification of work.[32]

Many claim that the ability to stop the line also represents an increase in the power and autonomy of the work force, and marks a radical departure from Fordism by reversing the relationship of workers to the line. According to this assumption, workers are no longer controlled by the line at Toyota, but are rather in control of it. However, the ability to stop the line has not alleviated the subordination of the Toyota work force to the mechanical pacing of production: because cycle times are so low and the work pace so fast, many workers have to stop the line just to keep up. According to Kamata, stopping the line was not an expression of power or autonomy, but rather an expression of desperation in trying to keep up with an unbearable work pace set by the "murderous conveyor."

Moreover, if a worker stops the line, the lost production time has to be made up through overtime. This implies not only extra work for the entire group, but also a drop in the production allowance wage (see below). As a result, there is significant peer pressure amongst the workers against stopping the line. Thus, while Toyota workers are indeed allowed to stop the line, doing so has serious negative consequences for the whole work group. Instead of stopping the line, workers are more inclined to keep up with it no matter what its speed, conforming to quality standards all the while. Ultimately, the ability to stop the line remains either a move of desperation to keep pace or an option not utilized because of its negative consequences. In either case it is hard to see line stopping as a tool of empowerment or autonomy.[33]

The JIT in-process quality control system has the final significant effect of tying the entire assembly line together in such a way that any mistake or defect disrupts the entire line. When a defect is produced, work at all downstream stations—towards final assembly—is disrupted because kanban orders cannot be filled until the defect is corrected, while work at all upstream stations is disrupted because production orders can't continue until the defect is corrected. This "precise coordination" of the production system also has serious implications for the Toyota work force, and it is to a discussion of these implications that the next section is directed.[34]

Peer Pressure

This total coordination of production, in conjunction with the kanban pull system, leads to the establishment of what Delbridge et al. refer to as the "customer ethos" at Toyota.[35] According to this arrangement, workers become customers of one another: subsequent

stations order components from preceding stations and thereby become the customers of the preceding stations. This relationship holds throughout the system and, as a result, each worker is both a producer for and a customer of other workers. Such relationships lead to the development of a regime of peer pressure at Toyota wherein keeping up with the line is not only necessary to satisfy management's production quotas, but is necessary to allow every other worker to fulfill his/her responsibilities. If one worker does not keep up, all of his/her fellow workers share in the consequences of disrupted production. Such consequences are several, and as a result of their magnitude the system of peer pressure is effective.

Primarily, although disrupted production delays the completion of each days production quotas, these quotas must be filled each day no matter how long it takes to do so. Therefore, when one worker delays production for the entire plant by falling behind the pace of the line, all workers are forced to work overtime until the production quotas are filled. Because of the impact that one worker's inability to keep pace has on the rest of the work force, peer pressure is directed towards keeping up with the line. Kamata expresses his experience of this situation in this way:

> If Fukuyama, the worker on my right, falls behind, he'll pull me behind, since I can barely keep up with the work myself. Even if Fukuyama finishes his job in time, should I take longer on my job, then the next worker, Takeda, will be pulled out of his position. It takes enormous energy to catch up with the line, and if things go wrong the line stops. That means overtime. So we do our job in a hell of a hurry to keep our fellow workers from suffering. That is how Toyota raises output.[36]

The minimization of the labor force contributes another element to the regime of peer pressure at Toyota. According to the JIT principle of minimization of resources, no extra workers are hired at Toyota to compensate for absenteeism. If a member of a team is absent, the team leader must therefore assume the absentee's duties on the production line. However, it is the team leader who is usually responsible for providing relief from work to production line workers, as well as for providing assistance in correcting quality problems. It is therefore impossible for the rest of the team to get any relief from work when the team leader has to work the line. This can preclude, for example, the

ability to leave the line even for a bathroom break, and if more than one team member is absent the results are even more dire. All of the burden of a worker's absence thus falls on the shoulders of the other production workers. While Toyota may cut costs by keeping the work force to a minimum, the price is clearly paid by the work force. Extreme peer pressure, this time directed against absenteeism, thus extends to pressure against taking sick days and vacation days allotted by the company.[37]

Peer pressure also arises as a result of the intersection of team organization and the Toyota wage system. In calculating wages, Toyota establishes a production allowance according to the amount of labor it takes a given team to reach its production quota. Wages increase as the team reduces the amount of labor—the number of workers multiplied by the total time taken—needed to reach its production goal. Thus, if one worker produces a defective component or falls behind the pace of the line, production gets delayed and the amount of labor needed to fill the production quota increases. This implies that the production allowance for the entire team will fall, and thus so will its wages. Again, individual mistakes or inability to keep pace with the line lead to negative consequences for other workers, and the result is pressure to produce without any mistakes at the breakneck pace set by management. In Kamata's words, "Everyone works desperately, hoping that he is not a burden to others. This is the 'relationship of a community bound together by a common fate.'"[38]

In conjunction with one another these elements compose a regime of peer pressure at Toyota. The result is increased pressure on workers to conform to production quotas, line speeds, and quality standards in a context of diminished managerial presence on the shop floor. That is, pressure to comply with management's objectives comes increasingly from the workers themselves. For management, this means an incredibly productive and cost-effective work force. For the workers, however, this means a grueling intensity of work with no chance to alleviate the pace.

3. PARTICIPATION WITHOUT POWER

Like the JIT system, the arrangements for employee participation at Toyota have received much attention, and are widely heralded as a great improvement over the Fordist system. At Toyota, employee suggestions on quality control and production rationalization are

actively sought by management through quality control circles. As reported in the literature, a quality control circle is a small group of employees who meet regularly under one supervisor to identify, analyze, and solve problems of product quality.[39] Circle members are ostensibly charged with deciding which production problems need addressing, investigating these problems, and developing solutions to them. Once an investigation has been carried out, findings and recommendations are presented to management, and if approved by management, these recommendations are carried out by the quality circle workers. In addition, management solicits employee suggestions through individual-based suggestion drives. Indeed, the claim is made that on account of these suggestion drives, Toyota workers are involved in the design and redesign of their jobs.

Quality circles and suggestion drives do expand workers' ability to contribute to the production process.[40] In a traditional Fordist plant, there are typically no such mechanisms for employee participation. At Toyota, however, as with the ability to stop the line, the ability to contribute to quality improvement and production rationalization does not amount to an increase in either worker power or autonomy for several reasons. First, with regard to both the quality circles and suggestion drives, workers can only make *suggestions*—they have no power to make or influence actual decisions. Before any changes in work organization, job design, or production design are made, they must be approved by management. This is true even for minute deviations from standard operating routines. Because management maintains total control over decision-making power within the firm, employee participation does not increase the power of the work force, nor does it increase workers' autonomy vis-a-vis management.

Second, the issues discussed by the quality circles and the range of suggestions sought during suggestion drives are not as open-ended as much of the literature claims. The agenda for quality circles is, in fact, largely set by management and oriented towards reducing costs and improving efficiency.[41] That is, employee suggestions are sought to increase the efficiency with which managerially determined goals are fulfilled. While the suggestion drives do seem more open-ended, Toyota management also delimits the agenda of these drives by using a "checklist of topics" when soliciting suggestions.[42] Without the power to determine the agenda for their participation, workers' ability to effect change that they desire, or that can improve their position within the firm is severely restricted.

Third, the criteria on which suggestions are approved or rejected is also set by management. Suggestions which can improve production

speed are thus more likely to be approved than those which improve working conditions at the expense of production efficiency. This again suggests that employee participation at Toyota amounts to a tool for furthering managerial goals, and does not increase the ability of workers to further their own goals. This paradox is reflected in the fact that the "improvements" in the production process that result from employee participation tend to intensify work. Without any power to set the agenda for changes, to decide which suggestions are approved, or to make any changes without management approval, it is unclear how quality circles or suggestion drives expand the power resources or autonomy of the Toyota work force.

The claim that workers are able to gain control over the design of their jobs through quality circles and suggestion drives is also clearly fallacious. As discussed above, jobs at Toyota are standardized to the point where each motion of each segmented task is prescribed by management through the standard operating routine sheets. If workers can come up with a way to shave a few seconds off their cycle times, and management approves, these changes may well be incorporated into a revised standard operating routine. However, the rigidity with which work is standardized, and the fact that absolutely no deviation from standard operating procedures can be made without management approval, suggests that workers are far from controlling their own work.

On the contrary, quality circles and suggestion drives may actually reduce the power resources that Toyota workers have compared to the situation in a Fordist plant. While Taylor certainly advocated appropriating worker knowledge in order to rationalize production, in the Fordist organization of work, there is a clear division between mental and manual labor wherein workers are not given any voice in the design of work. While this certainly and severely limits workers' power within the factory, it also leads to the development of a specific type of power resource. Through experience working on the shop floor, workers develop an intimate knowledge of production. Because managers are never involved in the manual side of production, management can never develop this knowledge on its own. Such intimate knowledge is, however, critical in the successful operation of an auto plant and therefore gives labor power vis-a-vis management, forcing management to allow workers some leeway in the way they do their work.

It is the work force's *exclusive* possession of this shop-floor knowledge that provides this resource. However, if this knowledge is transferred to management through quality circles or suggestion drives, the resource is lost. If management gains access to the intricacies of

production, they are not forced to grant workers leeway in the way they do their work, and can take even greater control over workers and the design of work.[43]

The situation at Toyota is thus one in which employees can participate only by allowing management to appropriate their knowledge in a drive to intensify work and extend managerial control. Contrary to much written on the subject, this does not amount to an improvement over the Fordist system in terms of either worker power or autonomy. Rather than improving on Fordism by increasing the power of the work force, Toyotism represents an improvement over the Fordist system in its ability to appropriate worker knowledge and institute managerial control. As Dohse et al. write:

> 'Toyotism' is not different from Fordism in its goal but in the way in which the goal is achieved. Even Taylor would have had no objection to rationalization suggestions from the employees. By contrast, he made every effort to get the aid of workers in rationalizing production. However, these efforts frequently failed because workers refused to cooperate. 'Toyotism' is, therefore, not an alternative to Taylorism but rather a solution to its classic problem of the resistance of the workers to placing their knowledge of production in the service of rationalization.[44]

4. CONCLUSION

This final point begs a final question: Why was management able to appropriate the knowledge of production line workers? More generally: Why was an organization of work based on the continual intensification of labor and the entrenchment of management control able to develop? We have seen why management was interested in developing a system of flexible production, and how different aspects of the system itself, including the regime of peer pressure and the wage structure, contributed to the success of this model. But these factors do not explain why the Toyota system itself was able to develop.

In his essay on "Product and Labour Strategies in Japan", Koichi Shimokawa argues that the establishment of the Toyota system was predicated on the development of cooperative relations between labor

and management. He writes, "It was only after the establishment of this cooperation that the . . . 'just-in-time' (JIT) system materialized."[45] Indeed, it is only through the "cooperation" of the labor force that this system of work organization is possible. Only because the Toyota labor union was willing to subordinate the interests of its workers to the goals of the firm was Toyota able to impose this system. Were the union to have fought for job rules, management would not have had the unlimited power to reassign workers at will, and thus the requisite labor mobility would be lost. Firm job rules would have also prevented the continuous rationalization of work, and the subsequent continuous speed-ups that mark the core of the JIT system. Were the union to have protected shop-floor knowledge of production, forced self-imposition of speed-ups would not have been possible. Were the union to have opposed a wage and promotion system based on production allowances and managerial discretion, the regime of peer pressure could have been avoided. The Toyota union, however, engaged in none of these struggles, giving management the free hand it needed to impose the system of work organization it understood as ideal. This union cooperation came, as we've seen, not out of any reconciliation of interests between labor and management, but out of the bitter defeat suffered by the labor movement in the early 1950s.

NOTES

1. There is an important distinction between numerical flexibility and functional flexibility. Numerical flexibility implies the firm's ability to easily increase or decrease its productive output by altering the number of workers employed. Toyota secures this numerical flexibility through the employment of seasonal or temporary workers, and through the subcontracting of work. During downturns in demand, for example, seasonal workers are released or not hired, and orders from Toyota subcontractors are reduced, causing workers at the subsidiaries to lose their jobs. Through numerical flexibility Toyota manages flexibility of production levels while offering "life-time" employment to its "regular employees." While numerical flexibility is critical to the Toyota management system, here I discuss only functional flexibility— as explained below—because it is this flexibility which is directly involved in the organization of work. I use the term flexibility to imply functional flexibility from here on.

2. Knuth Dohse, Ulrich Jürgens, and Thomas Malsch, "From 'Fordism' to 'Toyotism'? The Social Organization of the Labor Process in the Japanese Automobile Industry," *Politics and Society* Vol 4, No 2 (November, 1985), p. 119.

3. Mike Parker and Jane Slaughter, *Choosing Sides: Unions and the Team Concept* (Boston: South End Press, 1988).

4. Yasuhiro Monden, *Toyota Production System: Practical Approach to Production Management* (Atlanta: Industrial Engineering and Management Press, 1983), p. 72. It should be noted that this line balancing requirement is a problem in any serial flow production line system of work organization, not just at Toyota. In a sense, the need to standardize work in order to balance the line is a requisite of any assembly line system where management is interested in preventing idle time of labor. In this sense, the move away from the assembly line at Volvo's Kalmar and Uddevalla plants, discussed in Chapter Six, facilitates the move away from standardized work.

5. Satoshi Kamata, *Japan in the Passing Lane: An Insider's Account of Life in a Japanese Auto Factory*, Op cit., p. 104. (Satoshi Kamata was a production line worker at Toyota in Japan) At Toyota, cycle times are in the one to two minute range. In a cycle this short, only a very small fraction of a complete car can be assembled. See Kamata, pp. 29 and 206.

6. Monden, p. 87.

7. Monden, p. 89. See p. 90 for an example of a work sheet.

8. Kamata, p. 42.

9. As discussed in Chapter Three, Ohno had instituted the distinction between the "operating time of a machine" and the "working time of its operator" in order to increase the amount of time workers were actively employed. This required that Toyota workers be able to work five or ten different machines. As I will elaborate below, multi-machining not only facilitates flexibility, but also allows an increase in work intensity. Cusumano, *The Japanese Automobile Industry*, Op cit., pp. 273-274.

10. Monden, p. 112.

11. Kamata, pp. 87-88 and 103. Another part of the debate on multi-skilling has to do with the extent to which job rotation actually occurs within the factory. Most reports of the Toyota system put significant emphasis on job rotation and multi-machining. Kamata, however, reports a lack of rotation, at least amongst seasonal and temporary workers. In either case, it is clear that job rotation and multi-machining do not amount to multi-skilling.

12. Cusumano, p. 232.

13. A good diagrammatic representation of U-shaped production design can be found in Monden, p. 100, Figure 8.2.

14. There are numerous accounts of the kanban system. See, for example, Richard Schonberger, *Japanese Manufacturing Techniques: Nine Hidden Lessons in Simplicity* (New York: The Free Press, 1982), pp. 219-226; Cusumano, pp. 287-291; Monden, p. 17; Robert Hall, "The Toyota Kanban System," in Sang M. Lee and Gary Schwendiman, eds., *Management by Japanese Systems* (New York: Praeger Publishers, 1982), p. 145.

15. In an ideal JIT plant there would be zero work-in-progress inventory. This would be achieved by having only one withdrawal and one production ordering kanban between each two work stations. In actual Toyota plants more than one kanban is used between each station and, according to the number used, the amount of work-in-progress stored at outbound stock points is determined. The goal is to use as few kanbans as possible and to reduce the number through continuous rationalization of the production process.

16. Schonberger, p. 34.

17. Rick Delbridge, Peter Turnbull, and Barry Wilkinson, "Pushing back the frontiers: management control and work intensification under JIT/TQM factory regimes," *New Technology, Work and Employment* 7/2 (Autumn 1992), p. 99.

18. Hall, pp. 146-147.

19. Monden, pp. 120-121. While the identification and elimination of "wasted motions" is part of Taylorism and Fordism, the *continuous* process of identification and elimination is new with Toyota. In fact, by establishing work rules and job classifications, Fordist unions effectively prevent such continuous rationalization. The absence of such rules at Toyota—itself the product of the ineffectual enterprise unions which emerged out of the defeat of the early 1950s—gives management the flexibility to continuously rationalize work.

20. Kamata, p. 206.

21. Kamata, p. 199.

22. Kamata, p. 35.

23. Kamata, pp. 22-29.

24. Delbridge et al., pp. 103-104; Parker and Slaughter. p. 19.

25. Dohse et al., p. 136.

26. Christian Berggren, *Alternatives to Lean Production*, Op cit., p. 33.

27. At least in some Toyota plants, there are actual quotas set as to the number of suggestions workers must make. See Kamata, p. 150.

28. Kamata, p. 97-98.

29. Cusumano, pp. 320-322.

30. In his explanation of the in-process quality control system, Schonberger uses a metaphor with good explanatory value. He explains that in the Fordist system buffer inventories are much like water which covers "dangerous rocks." When buffer inventories are removed, these rocks (defects) are exposed. While such exposure makes the rocks more dangerous, it also allows them to be safely negotiated. Likewise, by exposing production problems at their source, it becomes possible to correct problems before they become built into final products. Schonberger, pp. 27-28.

31. Monden, p. 143.

32. Dohse et al., p. 130; Hall. p. 148.

33. See, for example, Dohse, et al., p. 133.

34. Cusumano, p. 276.

35. Delbridge et al., p. 102.

36. Kamata, p. 48.

37. Parker and Slaughter, pp. 21-22.

38. Kamata, pp. 201-202.

39. Jo Ann Hranac and Kathleen C. Brannen, "The What, Where, and Why's of Quality Control Circles," in Lee and Schwendiman, Op cit., p. 67.

40. Mike Parker, *Inside the Circle: A Union Guide to QWL* (Boston: South End Press, 1985), pp. 9-10.

41. Robert M. Marsh, "The Difference Between Participation and Power in Japanese Factories," *Industrial and Labor Relations Review* Vol 45, No 2 (January, 1992), p. 251.

42. Although this checklist does include such questions as "Are the lighting, ventilation, and temperature conditions good?," there are also a series of questions clearly devoted to rationalization. Monden, p. 127.

43. See, for example, Parker and Slaughter, p. 19.

44. Dohse et al., p. 128.

45. Koichi Shimokawa, "Product and Labour Strategies in Japan," in Tolliday and Zeitlin, eds., *The Automobile Industry and its Workers* (New York: St. Martin's Press, 1987), p. 233.

Chapter Six
The Volvo Model of Work Organization

The Japanese production philosophy may be said to have solved several of the difficulties Fordism met in an ever more changeable market. But other problems, especially those concerning working conditions in auto manufacturing, were largely unaddressed. Because of the social conditions under which Toyotism developed, these issues have not had priority. By contrast, such questions have been central to developments in Swedish auto companies in the 1970s and 1980s.[1]

Like Toyota in Japan, Volvo represents the most evolved example of work reorganization in Sweden. While Saab-Scania, the other major Swedish automobile manufacturer, has engaged in work reform, reforms at Saab were not as extensive as those developed at Volvo. As such, Volvo provides the best comparative model. While the core features of the Toyota system had developed together largely as a coherent whole by the 1960s, however, the Volvo model of work organization evolved through several distinct stages. I have chosen to discuss the first and last of these stages because they present the most significant changes in work design, and also convey the evolutionary character of Volvo's work reorganizations. In the first section of this chapter, I discuss the earliest of these reorganizations by presenting a description of Volvo's Kalmar plant. In the next section I discuss the Uddevalla plant, which represents the apex of the Volvo model and displays the clearest and most radical departures from the Fordist organization of work.

In Chapter Four, I discussed the pressures which led to the changes in work organization at Volvo. While it would be careless to posit that the two stages of work reorganization represented by Kalmar and Uddevalla correspond exactly to different stages in the progression of such preconditions, it does seem clear that as the movement for industrial democracy evolved, so did the nature of the work changes.

Briefly, again, the earliest pressure for change came as a result of labor militancy in the late 1960s in conjunction with increasing rates of absenteeism, labor turnover, and recruitment difficulties. Following these developments, Volvo engaged in its first phase of job redesign at the Kalmar plant. Taking place before the enactment of codetermination legislation, however, the reorganization was largely management led.

With the evolution of the post-Fordist international economy, however, Volvo management faced continued pressure for restructuring the organization of work in the 1970s and 1980s. Due to the continued strength of the labor movement, and the hegemony of social-democratic values, moreover, unemployment remained exceptionally low in Sweden throughout the 1970s and the 1980s, and as a result, the problems of absenteeism, turnover, and recruitment persisted through these two decades.[2] More importantly, the MBL codetermination legislation was passed into law after Kalmar. The MBL law was passed in 1977, and when a codetermination agreement was signed between Volvo and the Metall union in 1983, the union secured a role in the planning of all work changes. It was the new union power to shape the reorganization of work, in conjunction with the pressures of the post-Fordist international economy, which shaped the radical work reorganizations at Uddevalla.

1. KALMAR

Planning and Development

The Kalmar plant was the first major stage of job redesign at Volvo. Constructed in 1974, the new plant was designed in order to "humanize" work, as a clear response to the labor problems of the late 1960s and the early 1970s. The planning of the Kalmar production system was the responsibility of a development committee made up of representatives from Volvo, having no representatives from Metall, the auto workers union.[3] According to Berggren, Kalmar was "almost completely a product of management thinking. In no way did the unions influence or even participate in decisions pertaining to its design and technology."[4] As a result of the exclusion of the union from the development committee, management had significant leeway in making the work changes it desired. This does not, however, imply that the situation preceding Kalmar was equivalent to the conditions which gave rise to the changes at Toyota. Although Metall was not given a voice

in the design of Kalmar, it was the strength of the labor movement in Sweden which forced this reorganization of work. This implied that the changes at Kalmar had to be, to some extent, directed towards the improvement of the work process.

With management at the helm of the project, there were five main elements planned for the Kalmar production system. First, in a marked departure from the traditional assembly line, car bodies were to be propelled through assembly on carriers known as automatically guided vehicles (AGVs). Each car would be held on its own carrier, thus breaking up the assembly line. The AGVs were to be guided through the plant on magnetic tape inlaid into the factory floor, and controlled by a central computer. AGV assembly was also designed to allow workers to work on stationary carriers. Second, all workers at Kalmar were to be organized into working groups charged with the assembly of one of the car's functional subsystems—the exhaust system, the electrical system, etc. Third, interchangeability of skills within each group was to be ensured in order that group members could design job rotation for their groups.[5] The fourth goal, in marked contrast to the Toyota system, was the provision of buffer zones within the factory designed to allow working ahead or behind the pace of the line. This provision would allow workers to secure break time, and could potentially ensure that work was not dictated totally by the speed of the AGVs. Finally, the working environment at Kalmar was to be an improvement over all other assembly plants.[6]

The Early Years

Many of these goals were met during the first few years of production at Kalmar. Production was organized according to a flow of AGVs throughout the factory, and the flow was broken up into 20 distinct work areas to allow group assembly. Assembly began on the upper of two levels of the factory, where each car body was placed on a separate AGV. Each AGV then moved from one group area to another where distinct functional assemblies—steering, interior, electrical systems—were done. After the AGV moved through all work areas on the upper floor, it moved to the lower level, where, while functional assemblies were being completed on the upper level, engines, gear boxes, axles, and exhaust systems were assembled on distinct AGVs moving through group areas. While serving as transport devices, the AGVs also became assembly platforms while work was being carried out. This allowed workers the potential to perform their work on

stationary objects, in contrast to the situation in plants with traditional assembly lines.[7]

Kalmar scholars argue that the shift from assembly line to AGV production marked a radical break from the Fordist system. In the words of Ellegård, Engström, and Nilsson, "In Volvo's Kalmar plant, built in 1974, the assembly line was split up, having been the symbol of car factories since their introduction at Ford at the beginning of this century."[8] The shift away from the assembly line is not only significant in itself, but in the additional, more radical, changes in the nature of work that this shift facilitates. As discussed in Chapter Five, line balancing problems are endemic in any assembly line system and, as such, the assembly line demands a standardization of work restrictive of worker control and autonomy. Breaking up the line opened the door for the evolution of non-standardized, integrated production work based on whole car assembly, which would eventually afford the work force increased control and autonomy at Uddevalla.

At Kalmar itself, however, although the assembly line was broken up by the use of AGVs, production control remained in the hands of management. Such centralized control in a decentralized production process was achieved through a central computer—in the hands of Volvo management—which dictated the flow of the AGVs. Each AGV moved automatically to the next stop on its tour through the factory after three to four minutes. The movement of the AGVs was not dependent on whether or not a worker had completed his/her task and, as such, the Kalmar work force was still subordinated to the mechanical pacing of the production flow. This prevented, to a great extent, the work groups from gaining control over the way in which assembly work was done. Thus, although SAF argued that group work organization decentralized Kalmar, centralized control was still firmly entrenched and worker autonomy still severely restricted.[9]

Further, while the move away from the assembly line facilitated changes which would eventually increase worker power and autonomy, it also made a new form of work intensification possible. As discussed in Chapter Five, the traditional assembly line produces balancing problems in which workers are not employed at all times. Such pauses, though problematic from the managerial standpoint, provide short moments of rest for the work force. Breaking up the assembly line, however, makes possible the elimination of these short waiting periods. As such, the intensity of work can increase.[10]

There were, however, benefits gained by Kalmar workers as a result of the AGV system. Perhaps most importantly, the new organization of work extended cycle times considerably. Because the length of a work

cycle determines the breadth of job content, as discussed in Chapter Five, extending cycle times enlarges job content and increases the portion of the final product contributed by each worker. Longer cycle times may thereby facilitate increased identification with the final product and, in this way, increase the satisfaction to be gained from production work. As we saw, cycle times at Toyota were around one minute long, and could be reduced to even less than one minute through the continuous rationalization process. While cycle times at Volvo's traditional plants were only in the 2-3 minute range, a significant increase was secured at Kalmar.[11] Although AGVs moved after only 3-4 minutes, each Kalmar worker followed an AGV through four or five stations. Indeed, reported cycle times at Kalmar reached 25-30 minutes.[12]

Another positive element of the early Kalmar system was the provision of physical areas within the plant where workers could build up buffer stocks of assigned assemblies in order to earn break periods. By working ahead of the production rate for a period of time, workers could rest until their buffers had been depleted. These buffer zones also facilitated a work pace not totally dictated by the mechanical flow of the AGVs. According to Berggren, by instituting these buffer zones between each work area, the buffers also gave each group "temporal autonomy" from one another.[13] The extent to which the buffer zones were fully utilized in these ways seems to be a matter of some debate, however. In its report on Kalmar, an SAF-LO council noted that while the buffer zones were at times used for working ahead, they were often used to deal with production disturbances. While this use may have made the production system more resilient, when buffer zones were used in this way they would not have been available for storage of buffer stocks accumulated by working ahead of the production pace.[14]

Further, the organization of work at Kalmar resulted in an increased flexibility of production. By breaking up the assembly line, changes in production demands could be met more easily simply by using a greater or lesser number of carriers in response to increasing or decreasing levels of demand.[15] Because the carriers' flow through the factory was guided by conductive tape, moreover, it was easy to re-route and alter production. Simply by removing old tape and installing new tape a completely different assembly design could be achieved, allowing fast responses to changes in model demand.

Beyond the reorganization of production through the AGV carrier system, Kalmar also departed from traditional work organization through the implementation of group work. Because group work on a plant-wide basis was a primary goal of the Kalmar planners, the Kalmar

building was designed to facilitate group assembly. The building is constructed as a series of conjoining hexagons which provide a multitude of walls and corners, allowing each group its own clearly delineated production space. There are twenty distinct work areas at Kalmar, and in each work area there is a group of 15-20 workers.

Two primary elements of group organization at Kalmar in the early years need to be investigated. The first of these is the extent to which groups had control over their work, the power to make decisions on matters concerning the group, and autonomy vis-a-vis management. The power of the groups at Kalmar was, in fact, fairly restricted, although some discretion was granted. For example, groups were able to decide on the distribution of jobs among group members, the organization of materials, and at what pace work was to be carried out within the framework of the centrally controlled AGV pace (i.e., whether or not to work ahead for breaks). Perhaps most importantly, however, groups had some ability to change the method by which work tasks were carried out, marking an improvement over the rigidly standardized work routines at Toyota.[16] It is clear, nonetheless, that the power resources available to Kalmar groups were limited, as was their autonomy vis-a-vis management, primarily due to the centralized control of production. Moreover, groups were given no decision making authority in matters of production design or work organization.[17]

The second important element of group organization at Kalmar was the nature of the work for which each group was responsible. In the initial stages of Kalmar's operation, as we've seen, groups were organized around the assembly of functional components of the car. Because functional assemblies constitute something of a complete product, and certainly a more complete product than assemblies in traditional factories, functional assembly can facilitate greater identification with the product and thus increase the meaning and satisfaction of work. Group work at Kalmar was also defined by job rotation. Although much of this rotation, as at Toyota, involved switching between several similar and unskilled tasks, there was also rotation between assembly and pre-assembly work at Kalmar which allowed something of a varied work pace, as pre-assembly work tends to be less demanding than assembly work itself.

Finally, in addition to changes in production design and the organization of workers into groups, Kalmar made significant strides in improving the working environment. Perhaps most significantly, the AGVs which carried car bodies were designed to tilt 90°, thereby allowing easy access to the underside of the car body. This eliminated much of the strenuous bending involved in traditional auto assembly,

and allowed almost all work to be done in a standing position. AGVs on the lower level which carried engine assemblies, etc. were equipped with electronic lifting mechanisms which also eliminated the need to bend. Further, because the design of the factory building allowed each work group to be located against an outside factory wall, each group had access to a large outside window and lighting conditions in the factory were improved. Kalmar was also equipped with noise absorbent ceilings to cut down the high level of noise associated with auto manufacture. According to the SAF-LO council, 83% of workers at Kalmar in 1976 were satisfied with the "physical heaviness of work," 86% were satisfied with the lighting of the factory, 80% with the noise level, 55% with working positions, and 83% with "working areas and workplaces" in general.[18]

Rationalization and Retrenchment

While Kalmar witnessed neither the democratization of working life nor a significant transfer of control from management to labor in the first years of production, some significant changes and improvements were made. The lack of union influence in the design of the Kalmar project and in the project's future, however, were to become costly. A 1977 slump in the automobile industry hit Volvo quite hard, and Kalmar's production fell to barely half of its capacity. Management subsequently led an intensive rationalization of the work and production system, ostensibly to ensure that Kalmar survived this downturn, but it was again management that had control over the decisions made and the changes implemented. Work times were rationalized, and using a new work analysis system known as MOST, nearly all idle time was eliminated, implying an intensification of work. Centralized control of the AGVs was intensified through the introduction of a new computer monitoring system which checked the status of each AGV every five seconds.[19] By 1985, Kalmar even had a visual display unit in the control center which conveyed information to management on all operations in the plant.[20]

Many of the changes implemented in the early years of Kalmar, moreover, were abandoned in the years following 1977. With the introduction of JIT-like principles of materials minimization, use of the buffer zones was restricted, implying a further restriction on working ahead to earn break time and varying the pace of production.[21] The restrictions placed on the buffer zones also made group organization less effectual, as the buffers had provided autonomy between groups. Further, as demands for product variety increased, the possibility for

workers to do stationary dock assembly was eliminated due to the difficulty of storing a multitude of parts by each stationary AGV. The improvement over moving assembly was thereby lost. Kalmar groups also lost the ability to assemble one functional component of the car because rapid production changes had affected unevenly the content of each of these components. As a result, "The content of the team's work came to be defined, in conventional fashion, as a number of minutes, rather than functionally."[22] Finally, the wage system at Kalmar came to incorporate a results-based portion, tying workers' wages to the productivity of the plant. Although this portion accounted for a small percentage of the total wage, and was certainly nowhere near the 50% level of the Toyota wage system, the Kalmar system does tie individual performance to the wage of the entire work force. As such, it can lead to the development of peer pressure directed towards meeting production goals.

After a downturn in the demand for cars, management, who had developed the Kalmar system in the first place, was in a position to reverse much of what it had done: although the early Kalmar experiment had humanized the production process to some degree, it did not shift decision making power away from management and towards the workers. While the majority of Kalmar workers still felt that work was better at Kalmar than at traditional plants in 1985, and while the increased job content was "appreciated" by the work force, there was a high degree of dissatisfaction with Kalmar.[23] According to turnover statistics in 1985, the changes made at Kalmar were not significant enough to solve one of the primary problems that had led management to engage in the reorganization in the first place. This is reflected in the "Attitude Survey" taken by the SAF-LO-PTK Efficiency and Participation Development Council in 1985. Of 39 production workers asked if they were able to decide for themselves how to do their work, only 1 answered "completely," and only 9 answered "much," while 22 answered "little," and 7 "not at all." When asked if they had the opportunity to use their training and skills, only 1 answered "many opportunities," only 6 answered "rather many," while 16 answered "rather few," and 16 "none."[24]

With the retreat following the slump of 1977, much of the promise of Kalmar had been lost. In the final assessment, Kalmar was not very successful in either humanizing work or in moving towards worker control on the shop floor. With the centralization of control over the assembly process, Kalmar remained fairly traditional in the division of power resources within the firm. Further, there was little change in the actual nature of work at Kalmar. While work cycles did expand

significantly, with implications for work-force identification and satisfaction with work, work at Kalmar remained relatively low skilled and repetitive. Although the expansion of the cycles made work at Kalmar less repetitive than at traditional plants with lower cycle times, the expansion was not significant enough to mark a qualitative shift towards skilled production.[25]

Despite Kalmar's failures, however, it did constitute a first step in the evolution of the Volvo model. The break up of the assembly line was a serious departure from traditional assembly design and, as we'll see, opened the door for more significant changes at Uddevalla. The group organization of work, although it did not lead to worker empowerment at Kalmar, later proved key in increasing the power and autonomy of the work force. The extended work cycles, moreover, would prove a first step towards the radical expansion of cycle time, to the point where the "professionalization" of auto assembly work would be feasible. In concluding his analysis of Kalmar, Berggren argues that Kalmar represents not simply a failure of the Volvo work reorganization project, but a first stage in the evolution of this project. "It [Kalmar] showed, as the first factory of its kind in the world, that there were feasible alternatives to the traditional rigid assembly line." When the unions secured influence in the design of work changes at Volvo, the evolution continued.

2. UDDEVALLA

Planning and Development

Volvo began planning a new factory in 1985, the first one to be built in Sweden since Kalmar was constructed in 1974. Much had happened at Volvo, and in Sweden, between 1974 and 1985 which influenced the design that was to take shape at Uddevalla. The Volvo LB plant, designed in the late 1970s, had made significant strides towards increased worker autonomy on the shop floor and towards an improved work environment. Cycle times at LB increased to 37-44 minutes, and workers gained control over the transport of the AGVs. Buffers were incorporated into the production system, allowing a varied work pace and team autonomy.[26] LB, however, marks only a mid-point in the evolution of the Volvo model, and here I focus on only the two end points of the Volvo evolution. If Kalmar was the first phase in this evolution, Uddevalla is (so far) the final phase.

By 1985, both Volvo management and the Metall union were committed to significant change for a variety of reasons. For management, the demands of the post-Fordist economy for flexible and variated production had become clear, and the small size of the Swedish domestic economy made it especially important for Volvo to be competitive in international markets. As such, the demands for flexibility were high, while the feasibility of achieving this flexibility with traditional production methods remained low. Management was also inclined towards more radical changes in work organization because the labor market conditions which had contributed to problematic absenteeism, turnover, and recruitment problems in the early 1970s, most importantly the exceptionally low unemployment rate of less than 3%, had extended into the 1980s. The changes made at Kalmar, and even those made at LB, were not sufficient to solve this dilemma posed by the tight Swedish labor market.[27]

The newly won union right to participate in the planning stages of work redesign was the other factor which led to the commitment to significant change in the mid-1980s. The lack of a union voice in the planning of the Kalmar plant contributed to the limited nature of the reforms made there, and allowed management the ability to engage in a series of rationalizations in the late 1970s which reversed much of the progress made. When MBL became law in 1977, the stage was set for union involvement in planning production changes. Because MBL was only a frame law, however, it was up to individual firms and the unions representing their work forces to sign actual codetermination agreements. Due to employer reticence, it was not until 1983 that a codetermination agreement was signed at Volvo. Once the 1983 agreement was signed, however, Metall secured a role in the earliest stages of planning. It was, by 1985, the conjunction of the demands of post-Fordism, the pressure of tight labor markets, and the newly included voice of the Metall union that led to Volvo's most radical departure from traditional auto assembly.

From the very start of the Uddevalla project, the Metall union was involved in the planning and design of the production system and the organization of the work force. Before the actual planning began, a "projection group" was formed with representatives from Volvo and the union. The union representatives were involved full time and were "participating, for the most part, on the same terms as other members" of the group.[28] Following this projection phase, actual planning began in April/May of 1985 with the completion of a pilot study. Kalmar's director of engineering had become director of the new project, and argued against qualitative changes in assembly work. He instead called

for a production design, similar to the Kalmar model, based on AGV carriers. According to this first proposal, 700 workers would have been involved in the production of one car, and work cycles would have been 1-2 minutes.

This pilot study clearly did not live up to the expectations that the unions and many Volvo executives had for significant change. Reflecting their new power in the planning process, the Metall union was able to reject this first proposal, arguing that it was not a significant enough departure from the Kalmar model. The union rejection was based, above all else, on a demand that work cycles in the new plant be at least twenty minutes long. Having rejected the proposals in the pilot study, the union took the initiative and set forth a series of its own demands including stationary dock assembly, worker control over the pace of production with no machine pacing, broad and varied work content with production workers assured the ability to do non-assembly tasks, and buffer capacity between work stations.[29]

Following the submission of these union demands, the planning for Uddevalla entered a second stage, and an alternative Uddevalla-Ultra proposal was presented at the end of 1985. According to this proposal, the Uddevalla plant would consist of eight independent production shops connected in a series, with each car passing through all eight shops before it was completed. Within each shop, most of the work on each car would be done at one station. Cycle times under the Uddevalla-Ultra plan would have been 15-20 minutes, and approximately 100 workers would be involved in the assembly of each car.[30]

Along with the development of the Uddevalla-Ultra proposal, according to Berggren, the second stage of planning also saw a shift in the nature of the planning process itself, from reconstructing old ideas (i.e. those of the Kalmar system), to the development of entirely new conceptions of auto assembly. In Berggren's words, "This endowed the process with an open-ended character and created an unusually large space for exploring the fundamental conditions for change."[31] The development of an innovative training program, started at Uddevalla before the plant opened, was integral to this shift. The program served as a forum for experimenting with new ways of organizing production, in addition to training workers in already existing methods. It was, of course, easier to experiment in the training center than in actual production shops. One of the most important insights gained through this training program was the feasibility of exceptionally long cycle times. As Berggren writes:

The training shop came to function as a sort of
laboratory for production development, in which
changes in production design were tested before being
introduced into the product shops. Accordingly,
practical tests in the training shop showed it was
possible, with an appropriate materials arrangement
and administrative system, to learn how to build cars
in considerably longer cycles than twenty minutes—
which earlier had been considered the absolute upper
limit for car assembly. Thereby, a critical restriction
on further development was overcome.[32]

An important contribution to the development of such long cycle
assembly also came in 1985, as the result of research done on
functional assembly. Researchers at the Chalmer's Institute of
Technology showed that a car could be divided into four functional
subsystems and, thus, assembly design could realistically be divided
into only four stages.[33] This indeed marked a radical departure from
traditional auto assembly, in which hundreds, if not thousands of
separate stages of assembly were required. The training shop and the
research on functional assembly had cleared the way for the next stage
in the planning of the Uddevalla plant.

Following a union rejection of the Uddevalla-Ultra proposal,
planning for *complete car assembly* began in 1986. In accordance with
the Chalmer's research, materials kits were devised which contained all
parts necessary for the complete assembly of a car. The kits were
divided into four groups, representing the four functional subsystems:
leads, drive line, decor, and interior. Production was to be organized
around six *parallel* work shops. This marked a departure from assembly
line production and the serial flow models employed in all other Volvo
plants, because in parallel assembly each production shop housed the
complete assembly of an automobile. This is very different than the
situation at Kalmar, where each car flowed through every shop, and
where, therefore, each shop was home to only one portion of total
assembly. While Kalmar had broken up the assembly line, this
Uddevalla plan did away with serial flow production itself through the
implementation of parallel shops.

According to this same proposal, each shop was to have four group
zones linked together in a series. Each car would move between each
zone and, as a result, each group zone was responsible for the assembly
of 1/4 of each car. As there were to be two groups in each zone,
approximately 20 people would assembly 1/4 of the car. This would

extend cycle times to one full hour, marking a tremendous improvement over the Kalmar system and traditional assembly.[34]

The Uddevalla planning process did not end here, however. The planners finally agreed that each worker would be part of the assembly of an entire car, and in January 1987 it was proposed that each group zone would assemble a complete car. Under this proposal just twenty workers—two groups—would be responsible for the complete assembly of a car. In January 1988, final steps towards complete car assembly were taken. Each group, rather than each group zone, was slated to assemble a complete car and assembly was to be completed in two steps, rather than in four. Within each of the six product shops, then, eight independent parallel assemblies would take place, corresponding to the eight groups within each shop. At Uddevalla, there would be 48 independent, parallel assemblies. Assembly was totally stationary, and *ten people would be responsible for the assembly of an entire car*.

The Uddevalla Model

This was the model of work and production organization ultimately adopted, and by the summer of 1989 three product shops had begun assembly according to this model.[35] In assembly shops 1, 2, and 3, there were eight groups, each responsible for the assembly of a complete car. Each car moved after half of the assembly was completed, but assembly work itself was done only at stationary docks. Each worker was responsible for assembly of at least one-fourth of the car. In the other three shops, however, there were ultimately 12 parallel assembly groups, and an entire car was assembled at one dock. Accordingly, 4-5 workers were responsible for the assembly of an entire car. The magnitude of the difference between this system and the Fordist and Japanese models should be quite clear.

Where Kalmar had failed to depart from the traditional organization of production work, Uddevalla succeeded. In marked contrast to Kalmar, there was no central control over the production flow at Uddevalla. As a result of the design of the assembly process itself, within each product shop the assemblers had control over the pace of production.[36] Because each car moved only once in the first three product shops, and in the other shops the car never moved at all, there was no "queue" system demanding the exact coordination of work paces.[37] The coordination of work times often led, as at Toyota, to the rigid standardization of work processes, and the control over the carrying out of work tasks by management. By eliminating the need to coordinate work in this way, the tendency towards the standardization of work was eliminated as well.

The Uddevalla planners also eliminated the need for the centralized control of the production pace by eliminating the serial flow system.

Cycle times at Uddevalla were also dramatically increased. Cycle times were reported to be 90 minutes long in shops 1, 2, and 3, while in shops 4, 5, and 6 cycle times were about two hours. In response to the new system of whole car production, moreover, a new technical language was developed for communicating production information. Communication systems in traditional auto plants consist of codes and numerical representations for components which tell individual workers how to carry out their individual part of the production process. As such, the traditional communication system gives no overview of the production process as a whole. Because Uddevalla demanded that workers participate in the manufacture of a complete product, a communicative information system which provided an overview of the complete assembly process was introduced. Among the elements of this language were the substitution of names for codes, and the accessibility of the entire production process to each worker.

Redesign at Uddevalla also incorporated a new form of group organization. Within each group, one member acted as the group representative, and was responsible for managing the group's daily administration, and for certain planning functions. The position of group representative rotated between group members, in contrast to the system at Toyota. This group organization was used in an attempt to flatten the hierarchy of firm management. Such flattening was partially achieved through the devolution of administrative, quality control, and some planning functions to the group level in conjunction with a corresponding elimination of low level management. This devolution of responsibilities fulfilled the union's goal, noted above, of ensuring that assembly workers are able to do indirect, non-assembly work.[38]

As was the case with Toyota, however, the devolution of responsibilities at Uddevalla, while increasing the power and autonomy of the groups, may have also led to an intensification of work. Work intensity at Uddevalla was, in fact, a major concern of the Metall union. With the elimination of the assembly line and the serial flow production concept, the micropauses associated with traditional assembly line work were eliminated as well, potentially facilitating an intensification of work. In response, Metall did not advocate a return to traditional assembly concepts, but instead worked to ensure that Uddevalla workers had access to non-assembly tasks, as well as to traditional production tasks. Because such off-line tasks are less demanding than assembly jobs, including them in job rotations can decrease the intensity of work.

Again, however, the availability of non-assembly work only reduces work intensity if it is done *instead of* assembly work, and not *in addition to* assembly work. This distinction became the focus of codetermination negotiations at Uddevalla. For the union, the main challenge was ensuring that enough workers were assigned to each group in order that non-assembly functions could be handled by some group members, while a sufficient number of other group members remained available to carry out the required production work. If an adequate number of workers were assigned to each group, integration of non-assembly tasks would indeed decrease work intensity. The union argued for "negotiated management by objectives" to ensure that resources, including employees, were co-determined to a level which would lead to an "acceptable level of job intensity with room for cooperation, communication, and breaks."[39]

It is important to note the distinction between the Uddevalla system of group work and the team concept employed at Toyota. As Sandberg et al. write:

> It is essential to make this distinction between the Japanese team concept and the Scandinavian group work, for the team concept is basically still a Taylorist one with a detailed division of labor, assembly-line production . . . strong roles for forepersons and discipline, a small role for unions, little autonomy for group decisions, and few buffers. All this results in very great pressure on workers. Workers are encouraged to develop their suggestions for rationalizing production—without being given control over their work or changing their work in the direction of integration of tasks.[40]

In contrast, Swedish group work, as practiced at Uddevalla, was based on very different premises. First, the goal of group work at Uddevalla was the assurance of "good work," as defined by a strong union. Groups at Uddevalla, moreover, were not only given responsibilities, but were given autonomy and decision making power as well, in clear contrast to the situation for teams at Toyota. At Uddevalla, both horizontal integration of tasks—wherein workers do assembly work, quality control, and maintenance—and vertical integration of tasks—wherein workers take on responsibilities previously in the domain of management—occurred. Because Uddevalla's work groups gained control over administrative responsibilities and some planning functions, they

secured a degree of autonomy vis-a-vis management and increased their
ability to make decisions in matters which affected their work lives.
Moreover, the replacement of serial flow production by parallelization
implied that peer pressure was not exerted by one group on another,
implying a further extension of group autonomy.

As noted above, training was also an integral part of the Uddevalla
model. All Uddevalla workers completed an initial off-line sixteen week
training course, during which they learned to assemble one-fourth of a
car. Total training time was sixteen months however, during which
time workers learned to assemble a complete car through on-line
experience. By conducting the initial sixteen week training course off
the assembly line, the training process was made much easier on the
work force itself. If workers are trained on the line during production,
the rest of the workers are forced to make up the time lost due to the
inexperience of the untrained worker. In this respect, by training
workers on the line, it is the work force itself which has to bear the
costs of training. Through off-line training this is avoided.

Perhaps more importantly, however, as training times increase,
workers become less interchangeable. In traditional assembly plants,
training consists only of learning a clearly regimented and standardized
task. The unskilled nature of assembly line work has meant that
workers have been easily replaceable and have had, as a result, very
little power vis-a-vis the firm. With training periods of 16 weeks to 16
months, each Uddevalla worker became a significant investment for
Volvo and, as such, was not interchangeable. This, accordingly,
increased the power of each worker vis-a-vis the firm.

Implications for the Work Force and the Union

With the abandonment of serial flow production, work at Uddevalla
came to be defined by long cycles and integrated tasks. The new
approach to production work ended the standardization and regimentation
that had for so long been associated with automobile assembly. With
the changing nature of work, changing expectations for the work force
developed, and greatly expanded opportunities for creative involvement
with the work were created. The demands of whole car production
created the opportunity for an understanding of the entire production
process, marking a radical break with Fordist and Toyotist systems.[41]
By facilitating such total-process understanding, the work process
became a forum for learning. More than just knowing the task
sequences involved in the production of an entire car, itself a radical
improvement over the Fordist and Toyotist organizations of work, the

Uddevalla model required each worker to understand the relationships between these different work processes and to possess the ability to solve problems which arose, not only in one or several regimented tasks, but in the building of the car as a complete entity.

This requirement implied a radical change in the relationship between the worker and the production process: the work process at Uddevalla required the reintegration of mental and manual labor. Not only were workers required to carry out extensive manual labor, but due to the nature of whole car assembly they were required to understand the production process in which they were engaged. Workers at Uddevalla, in the course of the extensive training period as well as through on-line experience, thus developed an extensive collection of manual skills—the ability to build an entire car—in addition to the intellectual understanding of the car production process. This dual development constituted the reskilling of automobile work. In Nilsson's words, "It is this variety of [manual] tools in combination with the individual's mental activity—in the form of an inner monologue in relation to the tasks—that is decisive in the development of an 'activity' into a professional skill."[42]

The reskilling which took place at Uddevalla, was of course, completely different than the "multi-skilling" discussed in relation to Toyota. Multi-skilling at Toyota, as we've seen, means simply the learning of more than one unskilled, regimented, and standardized task and, therefore, the understanding of the complete production process afforded by the Uddevalla process is neglected. Workers at Toyota develop neither the manual ability to create an automobile in its entirety, nor the understanding of how each individual process is related to the production process as a whole.

The reskilling, or professionalization, of auto work which did occur at Uddevalla afforded production workers the opportunity to develop knowledge and to integrate creative and intellectual capacities into their work, thereby addressing many of the complaints traditionally lodged against assembly work. The participation of each Uddevalla worker in the process of assembling a complete car, moreover, reduced the alienation of production workers from the product in which they invested their labor. Finally, as Uddevalla workers acquired the ability to understand and complete the assembly of an entire car, their skills became quite valuable to Volvo and, as such, the workers gained a significant power resource vis-a-vis management. Marking a fundamental departure from the situation at a Fordist plant and at Toyota, Uddevalla workers were not easily replaceable.

In concluding his book on the Swedish auto industry, Berggren sums up these accomplishments. He writes:

> From the worker's point of view, this [holistic, long-cycle work] implied much more than just increasing the number of parts to be screwed or bolted: it enhanced functional understanding and the sense of purpose and meaning, it created possibilities to vary the work pace and the working positions, and it increased their opportunities for social cooperation and interaction . . . When properly organized and supported by a committed management, integrated assembly creates opportunities for vastly extended problem solving, by enhancing the intellectual quality of the work and the transcendent reflection of the workers, which are not confined to the continuous improvement ('kaizening') of fragmented suboperations.[43]

While integration of tasks led to a radical transformation of work at Uddevalla, it also posed some dilemmas for the unions. Perhaps the most significant of these was with the blurring of lines between white and blue-collar responsibilities. With the vertical integration of tasks, i.e., the responsibility given to teams of assembly workers for both the planning and execution of production, came a blurring of the distinction between white and blue-collar workers. Because two different unions represented the formerly distinct work groups, this tendency posed a conflict of representational rights. During the planning of Uddevalla it was proposed that one union represent both blue and white-collar workers. Although this proposal was rejected, it illustrates the dilemma posed by the integration of tasks for unions divided along the lines of white and blue-collar.[44]

While increased control over the day-to-day features of working life and the increasingly satisfying nature of work may make the role of the union less apparent, this threat does not seem to be a critical one. Although there may well have been some conflict between commitment to the company and commitment to the union at Uddevalla, the union still had several crucial issues on which it needed to demand codetermination negotiations. Only the union and not individual workers could ensure, for example, adequate staffing levels or absentee replacements. Further, as Sandberg argues, the development of work changes at Uddevalla may have given the workers impetus to work

through their union in order to secure any future changes which may have been desired. Even at a plant as advanced as Uddevalla, it appears as though there is still a fundamental role for the union.[45]

3. CONCLUSION

This chapter points us towards an important conclusion. The conditions imposed by the crisis of Fordism and the demands of the post-Fordist international market have certainly placed new requirements on the organization of automobile production. From management's perspective, the reorganization of work has served the purpose of creating a flexible production system demanded by the post-Fordist international economy. At Uddevalla, in a marked departure from even the Kalmar model, this was achieved through the parallelization of production. Because assembly was carried out at a number of different sites within the plant, rather than through one or several serial flows, variation in production patterns was easily facilitated. For example, mixed model production is easily achieved in the Uddevalla system by having some of the work stations completely assemble one model, while other stations assemble other models. Changes in the constitution of demand are also facilitated by parallel assembly. When a new model was needed, this change could be implemented at individual work stations without having to change the organization of an entire production flow. While the implications for workers may be layoffs, a change in the quantity of demand can be achieved by changing the total number of total work stations actively employed. If demand turns down, for example, several of the shops could be closed.[46] Finally, the nature of work at Uddevalla required workers not only to understand regimented tasks, but to understand the entire production process. As such, workers developed the ability to solve production problems, and thereby the ability to flexibly adjust to changing production demands.

Although flexibility may be demanded by economic conditions, the form that flexibility takes, and the system of work organization through which this flexibility is achieved, appears to be a product of the strength or weakness of labor. The comparative study of Volvo and Toyota indicates that demands for flexible production are filtered through national physiognomies, including the varying strength of each nations' class actors. In Sweden, the strength of labor, most recently channeled through the codetermination agreements of MBL, has forced Volvo to adopt a series of work changes which do not flow

deterministically from unstable markets and the demand for high product variation, but are the product of *both* economically determined managerial needs *and* union demands.[47] While the Toyota flexibility has been secured through the precise coordination of the production process, flexibility at Uddevalla was secured through the parallelization of production and the expansion of worker's skills.

Perhaps most importantly, the systems of work reorganization that result from the filtering of economic demands for flexibility through variable national physiognomies, have very different implications for workers. The system of work organization which facilitates flexibility at Toyota, the product of a weak and defeated labor movement, has contributed to the development of a regime of peer pressure, short cycle times, and a severe production pace. In contrast, the work organization which allowed flexibility at Volvo, developed in the context of strong unions, led to the extension of control and autonomy to the work force, as well as contributing to the reskilling of auto assembly work.

NOTES

1. Christian Berggren, *Alternatives to Lean Production*, Op cit., p. 56.

2. For example, in 1985 the unemployment rate in Sweden was 2.8%, compared to 9.3% in Germany and 7.2% in the U.S. Berggren, p. 73. Table 4-1.

3. It appears as though no non-union representatives of Volvo workers were included in the planning stages either. Auer and Riegler state that the implementation of Kalmar design was carried out by a project committee made up only of managers, production technicians and architects. Although there were union representatives on a committee involved in approving the design of work at Kalmar, the unions were totally excluded from the development committee itself. See Peter Auer and Claudius Riegler, *Post-Taylorism: The Enterprise as a Place of Learning Organizational Change — A Comprehensive Study on Work Organization Changes and its Context at Volvo* (Stockholm: Arbetsmiljöfonden (The Swedish Work Environment Fund), 1990), p. 24.

4. Berggren, pp. 120-121. In fact, the lack of union influence in the planning stages of this experiment led LO to criticize the experiment itself. See Bengt Abrahamsson, *Sweden: Industrial*

Democracy in the 1970s (Stockholm: Arbetslivscentrum (The Swedish Center for Working Life), 1980), p. 35.

5. The danger of this "goal" should be obvious from Chapter Five.

6. Phillip Bently, "Saab-Scania and Volvo Shop-Floor Changes," *International Series* No. 1 (September, 1974), pp. 23 and 27.

7. Work performed on AGVs while the carriers were in motion was known as line assembly, while work carried out on stationary AGVs was known as dock assembly. The work content was the same in both situations. Stefan Agurén, Reine Hansson, and K.G. Karlsson, *The Volvo Kalmar Plant: The Impact of new Design on Work Organization* (Stockholm: The Rationalization Council, SAF-LO, 1976), p. 11.

8. Kajsa Ellegård, Tomas Engström, and Lennart Nilsson. *Reforming Industrial Work —Principles and Realities: In the planning of Volvo's car assembly plant in Uddevalla* (Stockholm: Arbetsmiljöfonden (The Swedish Work Environment Fund), 1992), p. 8.

9. Åke Sandberg et al., *Technological Change and Co-Determination in Sweden* (Philadelphia: Temple University Press, 1992), p. 79.

10. Sandberg et al., p. 71.

11. Berggren, p. 194.

12. Auer and Riegler (1990), p. 25; Berggren, pp. 123-126.

13. Berggren, p. 121. Such temporal autonomy of work groups may pose a threat to worker collectivity within the plant. While it appears, as Berggren seems to argue, that such autonomy increases workers' ability to control the work process, the division of workers into groups may also hinder solidarity within the factory.

14. Agurén et al. (1976), p. 23.

15. Adding carriers, without a corresponding increase in the work force, would clearly lead to an intensification of work.

16. Agurén et al. (1976), p. 27.

17. Sandberg et al., p. 73.

18. Agurén et al. (1976), p. 34.

19. Berggren, p. 123.

20. Stefan Agurén, Christer Bredbacka, Reine Hansson, Kurt Ihregren, and KG Karlsson *Volvo Kalmar Revisited: Ten Years of Experience* (Stockholm: Efficiency and Participation Development Council, SAF-LO-PTK, 1985), p. 74. PTK is the Swedish Office Employees' Negotiating Unit.

21. Auer and Riegler (1990), p. 27. Agurén et al. (1985) report, however, that it was still possible to work ahead and earn breaks at Kalmar as late as 1985.

22. Berggren, p. 127.

23. Agurén et al. (1985), p. 12; Sandberg et al., p. 72.

24. Agurén et al. (1985), pp. 95 and 103.

25. Auer and Riegler (1990), p. 27.

26. Berggren, p. 132.

27. Berggren, p. 232.

28. Ellegård et al., p. 12.

29. Sandberg et al., p. 87; Berggren, p. 148.

30. Ellegård et al., pp. 16-17.

31. Berggren, p. 150.

32. Berggren, pp. 150-151.

33. Berggren, p. 151.

34. Another important development took place around this time. A joint labor-management group visited a Nissan plant in the U.K. in order to assess the Japanese model of work organization. The group rejected the Japanese model, which further strengthened the commitment to finding a new road to work innovation. See Berggren, p. 146.

35. Ellegård et al., pp. 17-20; Berggren, pp. 151-153.

36. Auer and Riegler (1990), p. 37.

37. Berggren, p. 162.

38. Ellegård et al., p. 23.

39. Sandberg et al., pp. 93 and 94. A final element of the team organization at Uddevalla deserves mention, especially in reference to the discussion of this issue in Chapter Five. In contrast to the many positive implications of the Uddevalla organization for workers (see below), teams were not provided with replacement workers if a group member was absent on sick leave or paternal leave. Workers have commented on pressure against taking such leaves for this reason. Clearly, this is an undesirable element of the Uddevalla system, and one with negative implications for workers, including the potential for the development of peer pressure on the shop floor.

40. Sandberg et al., p. 94.

41. Berggren, p. 162.

42. Ellegård et al., p. 39.

43. Berggren, pp. 242-243.

44. Auer and Riegler (1990), p. 22. (Metall is the union for blue-collar workers at Uddevalla, and SIF is the union for white collar employees in industry.) It is not clear whether this proposal was made

by management or by one of the unions. However, Auer and Riegler write that "in the end," the proposal was rejected "by all the trade unions," perhaps indicating that this was indeed a management proposal.

45. Sandberg et al., p. 273.

46. A parallel assembly system such as Uddevalla thus allows both numerical and functional flexibility.

47. In addition to its Swedish plants, two of which are presented here, Volvo also operated auto plants outside of Sweden. One of these plants is in Ghent, Belgium. At Volvo's Ghent plant, production is organized according to the traditional serial flow assembly line, and work is unskilled and repetitive. While a full discussion of the Ghent plant would not be appropriate here, I raise it as an example for the following reason. Outside Sweden, where unemployment is higher, where the labor unions are weak and do not have the codetermination rights secured through MBL, and where there is no solidaristic wage policy, Volvo has not engaged in any extensive experiments in work reorganization. See for example, Olle Hammarström and Russell D. Lansbury, "The art of building a car: the Swedish experience re-examined," *New Technology, Work, and Employment* (Autumn 1991), p. 87. The authors write, "It seems likely that only management faced with shortage of labour, union pressure and reduced wage differentials will be forced to be as imaginative as Volvo has been at Uddevalla." p. 88.

Conclusion

The basic problematic underpinning this book was the general crisis of the Fordist economic order, and the shift to post-Fordist international markets which increasingly demanded productive flexibility. This demand for flexibility required a reorganization of the work process in ways different from the Fordist system. With the crisis of Fordism and the continued success of Japanese industry, most notably its automobile manufacturers, a large number of people in business, government, academic, and even labor circles, argued that success in the post-Fordist economy depended upon adoption of the system of work organization used by these Japanese firms. In other words, to many it seemed like the Japanese model of work organization was *the* post-Fordist model of work organization. What this book has attempted to demonstrate, however, is that the Japanese model is but *one* alternative to Fordist production methods, and that there are other systems of work organization which are equally capable of achieving the flexibility demanded by post-Fordist markets. Perhaps most importantly, I have tried to show that different alternatives to Fordist work organization have very different implications for the post-Fordist work force.

In order to understand the divergent alternatives to the Fordist organization of work, as I have argued, it is necessary to understand the contexts in which these alternative systems evolved. As a window through which to view the evolution of non-Fordist work systems, I have explained the development of work reorganization in the Japanese and Swedish automobile industries. In both cases, a set of economic conditions brought pressure to bear on the automobile firms to develop flexible modes of production. In the Japanese case, these pressures came in the early 1950s as a result of a series of factors including the limited size of the Japanese domestic market, in conjunction with a demand for a diversified product line, the failure of the auto firms to successfully penetrate U.S. markets on the basis of price competition and the necessity for continuous product differentiation that grew out of this experience, and crises of costs and quality which plagued the industry in the 1950s. In Sweden, by contrast, the demands for flexibility came as a

result of the crisis of Fordism itself. The increasing instability of world markets called forth a system of work organization that was able to rapidly respond to changing market conditions. The small size of Sweden's home market and the country's high dependence on export markets exacerbated the demands of post-Fordism for Sweden's automakers.

While in both cases economic conditions necessitated flexible production and thus a reorganization of work, each work system evolved in the context of very different national physiognomies. Ultimately, as I have argued, it was the interaction between economic conditions and the strength of labor—supported or discouraged by the state—which forged the actual structure of these work systems. In the Japanese case, following a reversal of policy by the American occupation forces in the early 1950s, the state revoked its support for the unions, and granted it to business, organized under the aegis of the Nikkeiren federation. Following several years of labor militancy, business was able to launch an offensive which culminated in the strike of 1953. This strike resulted not only in the defeat of the most militant of the auto unions, Nissan's union, but in the defeat of the industrial union movement. For the Japanese auto firms, and especially Toyota, located as it was in a quintessential company town, this defeat effected the transition to an auto industry organized by ineffectual enterprise-based unions. These unions, dependent on the success of their individual firm and integrated into its managerial structure, failed to serve employee interests. This lack of union influence was evident in the development and implementation of work changes: lacking an independent voice, labor and labor's interests were totally excluded from the reorganization of work. Management, therefore, had a free hand in developing the work system which best met its needs in responding to the economic conditions outlined above.

In Sweden, by contrast, a social democratic labor movement, consisting of a strong and nationally organized labor union and a social democratic party in power for most of the post-war era, was able to influence the reorganization of auto work. In the post-war years, LO and the SAP were able to develop an economy based around full-employment and high levels of social welfare. Because these economic conditions survived through the 1970s, when employers where faced with the crisis of Fordism and the need to reorganize work, the auto firms were also faced with the need to alleviate problems of high labor turnover, absenteeism, and recruitment difficulties. The LO-coordinated solidaristic wage policy, moreover, restricted auto management's ability to circumvent these problems through high wage packets. By shaping

the economic environment, a strong Swedish labor movement forced management to incorporate labor's interests into the design of work changes.

While certainly important, the effect that the conditioning of the economic environment had on the design of work reorganization proved limited in scope. It was following a union-state drive for industrial democracy, culminating in the MBL law and subsequent codetermination agreements, that Swedish unions gained influence in the actual planning of work changes. Beyond shaping the economic environment, then, the codetermination agreements brought an independent labor voice to the planning stages of work reorganization. Through both means, the Swedish labor movement was able to force management to incorporate labor's agenda into the planning of the flexible, post-Fordist automobile plants.

The two systems of work organization which developed as a result of the conjunction of economic demands for flexibility and these very different degrees of labor strength, achieved flexibility in very different ways. At Toyota, the Japanese auto firm which went the furthest in redesigning work, flexibility was achieved through a production system based around standardization and regimentation of tasks, team work and job rotation among these standard tasks, inventoryless production, minimization of components and workers, continuous rationalization of work, and a thoroughly integrated production system. At Volvo—and most highly developed at Uddevalla—flexibility was achieved through the parallelization of production, the breakup of the linear flow assembly line, and group work based on skilled workers with functional knowledge of the assembly process.

While both systems facilitated flexible production, the ways in which this flexibility was achieved had considerably different implications for Toyota and Volvo workers. The system of work organization developed by an unfettered management at Toyota did not, as advertised, end the alienating, degrading, and monotonous nature of assembly-line work. Rather, flexibility was achieved in a system defined by the continuous intensification of work, complete managerial control over the work process and the deployment of the labor force, and an institutionalized regime of peer pressure. The nature of work also forbid worker identification with the completed product, and eliminated all worker power resources vis-a-vis management by deskilling all jobs and appropriating worker knowledge of the shop-floor production processes. This model of work organization also has significant implications for the formation of class consciousness and class struggle. The various mechanisms of the JIT system have allowed the

substitution of worker peer pressure for managerial intervention on the shop floor. While it is still clear that management sets production goals and the production pace, the regime of peer pressure intentionally realigns the pressure for production efficiency from a management-labor struggle to a labor-labor intensive effort. Work-force solidarity, encouraged under traditional Fordist systems and crucial to class consciousness formation and the struggle of workers and unions against managerial control, may be threatened by the Toyota system.

The Volvo system, as illustrated most clearly at the Uddevalla plant, has implied a very different set of factors for Volvo workers. With the break-up of the linear flow assembly process, and the practice of whole car assembly, Uddevalla workers became responsible for the assembly of complete cars. Their work was therefore less fragmented, less standardized, and more skilled than work in a traditional Fordist plant, or work at Toyota. The change in the nature of work gave Uddevalla workers the opportunity to integrate their mental, as well as manual capacities into the production process, and facilitated worker identification with the complete production process, and thus with the product itself. In this sense, the Uddevalla work organization lessened the alienating nature of auto work. Moreover, because of the breadth of the work for which each Uddevalla worker was responsible, extended training periods were necessary. The functional knowledge required of each worker implied the reskilling of auto work, and subsequently an extension of the power resources available to the work force. Group work at Uddevalla also incorporated a degree of vertical integration which implied greater power and autonomy vis-a-vis management for the Uddevalla workers. While work at Uddevalla was intensified through the elimination of micropauses inherent in linear flow systems, and posed problems for union organizational structure, it marked a clear break from, and a significant improvement over the Fordist system.

The critical variable in the evolution of the divergent systems of flexible work organization at Toyota and Volvo has thus been the strength of organized labor. Contrary to managerial claims aimed at securing union concessions, a strong labor movement and powerful unions do not inhibit the feasibility of flexible production and are thus not incongruous with success in the post-Fordist economy. What a strong labor movement and powerful unions do imply is a *very different version of flexible production, with very different implications for labor.*

A question which remains, however, is the extent to which the two systems provide feasible alternatives to Fordism on competitive grounds. It is clear that the Toyota system has been competitive in the

context of post-Fordism's destabilized international economy. In this sense, though implying a series of negative consequences for labor, the Toyota system marks a feasible alternative to Fordist production. In terms of economic feasibility, although it is not possible to do a full evaluation, the Uddevalla system seems to have had the potential to become an alternative to Fordist production. It is very difficult to compare Uddevalla with Toyota, or with any other auto plant, in terms of economic data. As Berggren points out, there is much involved in securing high productivity levels besides the system of work organization. For example, Toyota's supplier system gives Toyota a great productivity advantage over Volvo, which lacks such an ancillary firm network. Moreover, the quality of the cars assembled in each plant, if different, could contribute to productivity discrepancies.[1] Thus while Japanese plants may outpace Volvo in terms of productivity levels, this does not imply that Uddevalla's system of work organization is not a feasible alternative to Fordist methods. Finally, Uddevalla was developed at a time of economic crisis, when the Swedish auto industry was in poor shape. As a result, the closing of Uddevalla may have had more to do with the weakness of the Swedish economy and the Swedish auto sector than with the work system itself.

While the evidence is fragmentary, and fairly non-conclusive at this point, there is some reason to believe that, in economic terms, the Uddevalla model could have eventually replaced the Fordist system. By 1991, Uddevalla had reached the productivity level of Volvo's main assembly plant, a plant which was still using traditional assembly line production methods. Turnover at Uddevalla was down to 4% by May 1991, and the quality index at Uddevalla was 910, according to a measurement system wherein 1,000 implies a "perfect car."[2] Moreover, Uddevalla was in operation only for a few years, and past experience indicates that plants which incorporate extensive innovation can take several years to reach their productive capacity. Having made significant strides in raising productivity and quality levels, the Uddevalla work system incorporated potential for further improvements. As I argued in the preface to this book, the considerations involved in the decision to close Uddevalla went beyond—if they did not actually ignore— productivity and quality. At a time when labor input and cooperation, along with the capacity for productive flexibility seem the keys to competitive success, the Uddevalla model—which incorporated parallel production and drastically reduced lead times (see Preface)—held competitive promise.

The conclusions reached here, and throughout this book, have important implications for the way we think about post-Fordism and,

more specifically, the way we understand the role of labor in the post-Fordist economy. Beyond understanding the interaction of economic conditions and the strength of labor in forging divergent alternatives to Fordist production systems, these conclusions can shed light on the American situation. In facing the crisis of Fordism, American labor, to a large degree, seems to have accepted the argument that union strength is not compatible with efficiency. The argument has been that in order for American auto firms to achieve flexibility, unions have to concede the loss of job rules, etc. or face the closings of more and more auto plants. Where possible, U.S. makers have opened new plants, often in joint-venture with Japanese firms, in southern non-union states. But while the Japanese case indicates that the Toyota version of flexibility does indeed depend on a weak labor movement and ineffectual, virtually silent unions, the Swedish case shows that other versions of flexibility are available which are consummate with labor strength and vocal union demands.

In light of these options, American labor does not face a single, bleak future. The drive for flexibility, if able to occur in a context of continued union concessions to managerial demands, will indeed result in the promulgation of U.S. auto factories organized according to the Toyota model of flexibility, and thus according to the Toyota model of work organization. Already, at places like the GM-Toyota New United Motor Manufacturing, Inc. (NUMMI) plant in Freemont, California and the Ford-Mazda plant in Flat Rock, Michigan, as well as at Saturn plants across the sunbelt, the Japanese system of work organization is operant. Regardless of a sophisticated advertising campaign claiming the contrary, the situation for workers at these plants has mirrored the situation for Toyota workers in Japan outlined in Chapter Five.[3] High work intensity, continuous speed-ups, boring and repetitive work, complete managerial control, and peer-pressure define American plants organized around this work system, just as they define Toyota plants in Japan.

Without disputing the claim that American auto firms need to develop flexible production systems, American auto unions should note the Volvo case and the possibility for a different version of flexibility. In order for labor's interests to be incorporated into the planning of the new, flexible, work designs, the unions need to end the trend of concession granting and begin bargaining with Big Three management over the development of flexible work systems which serve the interests of both management and labor. While any form of flexibility might well require the relinquishing of union control over narrow job classifications, the U.S. auto unions' primary power resource on the

shop floor today, in return for the abandonment of job control unionism, the UAW can begin to demand work reorganizations more along the lines of the Volvo model. It is only in a context of labor strength and union demands, as I've argued, that a labor-inclusive model of flexible production will develop.

Of course, the U.S. labor movement is not nearly as organized or powerful as the Swedish movement, and the UAW lacks the organizational density and resources of Sweden's Metall. Moreover, there is nothing approaching an American variant of MBL to mandate that management bargain with unions over issues concerning work reorganization. Without these resources it is unlikely that the American unions will be able to demand an American variant of the Uddevalla plant. However, the U.S. government, especially the Department of Labor under Secretary Reich, has shown an interest in developing flexible production systems to increase the competitiveness of American firms. Taking heed of not only the Japanese model, but the Swedish model as well, the government must realize that different versions of flexibility have very different implications for citizens who work in these new plants. As such, the state could encourage or legislate that firms bargain with unions over the nature of work reorganizations undertaken in the name of flexibility.

Even if the U.S. government does not strengthen the unions' position, American unions should use the resources they do have to fight for a more labor inclusive model of flexible production. While another Uddevalla may not be feasible in the U.S., the UAW is still stronger than the enterprise unions in Japan and should be able to secure a flexible work organization with implications less severe than those which follow from the Toyota model. Dissident locals, such as the New Directions union at Mazda Flat Rock, provide hope that American auto unions will raise some voice of protest, and demand some influence in the shaping of the new work systems. Without making any such demands, the unions will ensure that flexibility in America develops along the lines of the Toyota model. As this book shows however, this outcome is not pre-determined, and systems of work organization developed in the context of a strong union voice have the potential not only to meet the challenges of the post-Fordist economic order, but to do so in a way which restores satisfaction and dignity to the work process.

NOTES

1. Berggren, *Alternatives to Lean Production,* Op cit., p. 165. As an example, Berggren notes that in a 1988 experiment, engineers found that Honda doors could be built in 1/4 the time it took to build Saab doors, using "the same methods and technology."

2. Berggren, Pg 164.

3. See Parker and Slaughter, *Unions and the Team Concept,* Op cit.; Joseph Fucini and Suzy Fucini, *Working for the Japanese: Inside Mazda's American Auto Plant* (New York: The Free Press, 1990).

Bibliography

Abegglen, James C. and George Stalk, Jr. *Kaisha, The Japanese Corporation*. New York: Basic books, Inc., 1985.

Abrahamsson, Bengt. *Sweden: Industrial Democracy in the 1970s*. Stockholm: Arbetslivscentrum (The Swedish Center for Working Life), 1980.

Agurén, Stefan, Christer Bredbacka, Reine Hansson, Kurt Ihregren, and KG Karlsson. *Volvo-Kalmar Revisited: Ten Years of Experience*. Stockholm: Efficiency and Participation Development Council, SAF-LO-PTK, 1985.

Agurén, Stefan, Reine Hansson, and K.G. Karlsson. *The Volvo Kalmar Plant: The Impact of new Design on Work Organization*. Stockholm: The Rationalization Council, SAF-LO, 1976.

Amsden, Alice H. "Third World Industrialization: 'Global Fordism' or a New Model?" *New Left Review* 182 (July-August 1990).

Auer, Peter and Claudius Riegler. *Post-Taylorism: The Enterprise as a Place of Learning Organizational Change—A Comprehensive Study on Work Organization Changes and its Context at Volvo*. Stockholm: Arbetsmiljöfonden (The Swedish Work Environment Fund), 1990.

Bently, Phillip. "Saab-Scania and Volvo Shop-Floor Changes." *International Series* No. 1 (September, 1974).

Berggren, Christian. *Alternatives to Lean Production: Work Organization in the Swedish Auto Industry*. Ithaca: ILR Press, 1992.

Berggren, Christian. *Volvo Uddevalla—a dream plant for dealers?*.
Stockholm: Royal Institute of Technology Department of Work
Science, February, 1993.

Block, Fred. *Postindustrial Possibilities: A Critique of Economic
Discourse*. Berkeley: University of California Press, 1990.

Boyer, Robert. "New Directions in Management Practices and Work
Organization: General Principles and National Trajectories."
CEPREMAP, CNRS, EHESS (August, 1991).

Costello, Nicholas, Jonathan Michie, and Milne. *Beyond the Casino
Economy: Planning for the 1990s*. New York: Verso Press, 1989.

Cusumano, Michael. *The Japanese Automobile Industry: Technology
and Management at Nissan and Toyota*. Cambridge: Harvard
University Press, 1985.

Delbridge, Rick, Peter Turnbull, and Barry Wilkinson. "Pushing back
the frontiers: management control and work intensification under J
IT/TQM factory regimes." *New Technology, Work and
Employment* 7/2 (Autumn 1992).

Dohse, Knuth, Ulrich Jürgens, and Thomas Malsch. "From 'Fordism'
to 'Toyotism'? The Social Organization of the Labor Process in the
Japanese Automobile Industry." *Politics and Society* Vol 4, No 2
(November, 1985).

Drago, Robert and Terry McDonough. "Capitalist Shopfloor Initiatives,
Restructuring, and Organizing in the '80s." *Review of Radical
Political Economics* Vol. 16(4) (1984).

Edlund, Sten and Birgitta Nyström. *Developments in Swedish Labor
Law*. Stockholm: The Swedish Institute, 1988.

Ellegård, Kajsa, Tomas Engström, and Lennart Nilsson. *Reforming
Industrial Work—Principles and Realities: In the planning of
Volvo's car assembly plant in Uddevalla*. Stockholm:
Arbetsmiljöfonden (The Swedish Work Environment Fund), 1992.

Elvander, N. "Sweden." In Benjamin C Roberts, ed., *Towards Industrial
Democracy*. Montclair: Allanheld, Osmun Publishers, 1979.

Forsebäck, Lennart. *Industrial Relations and Employment in Sweden.*
Uppsala: The Swedish Institute, 1980.

Friedman, David. *The Misunderstood Miracle: Industrial Development
and Political Change in Japan.* Ithaca: Cornell University Press,
1988.

Glyn, Andrew, Alan Hughes, Alain Lipietz, and Ajit Singh. "The Rise
and Fall of the Golden Age." In Marglin and Schor, eds., *The
Golden Age of Capitalism.* Oxford: Clarendon Press, 1990.

Gordon, Andrew. *The Evolution of Labor Relations in Japan: Heavy
Industry, 1853-1955.* Cambridge: Harvard University Press, 1985.

Gourevitch, Peter, Andrew Martin, George Ross, Christopher Allen,
Stephen Bornstein, and Andrei Markovits. *Unions and Economic
Crisis: Britain, West Germany and Sweden.* Boston: George Allen
and Unwin. 1984.

Gourevitch, Peter. *Politics in Hard Times: Comparative Responses to
International Economic Crises.* Ithaca: Cornell University Press,
1986.

Gyllenhammar, Pehr G. *People at Work.* Reading Massachusetts:
Addison-Wesley Publishing Company, 1977.

Halberstam, David. *The Reckoning.* New York: William Morrow and
Company, Inc., 1986.

Hall, Robert. "The Toyota Management System." In Sang M. Lee and
Gary Schwendiman, eds., *Management by Japanese Systems.* New
York: Praeger Publishers, 1982.

Hammarström, Olle and Russell D. Lansbury. "The art of building a
car: the Swedish experience re-examined." *New Technology, Work,
and Employment* (Autumn, 1991).

Heclo, Hugh and Henrik Madsen. *Policy and Politics in Sweden:
Principled Pragmatism.* Philadelphia: Temple University Press,
1987.

Higgins, Winton. "Industrial Democracy and the Control Issue in
    Sweden." In Ed Davis and Russell Lansbury, *Democracy and
    Control in the Workplace*. Australia: Longman Cheshire, 1986.

Himmelstrand, Ulf, Göran Brulin, and Richard Swedberg. "Control,
    Motivation, and Structure: The 'New Managerial Philosophies' vs.
    Industrial Democracy." *Economic Analysis and Workers
    Management* 1, xx (1986).

Hirst, Paul and Jonathan Zeitlin. "Flexible Specialization vs Post-
    Fordism: Theory, Evidence, and Policy Implications." *Birkbeck
    Policy Centre Working Paper* (May, 1990).

Hranac, Jo Ann and Kathleen C. Brannen. "The What, Where, and
    Why's of Quality Control Circles." In Sang M. Lee and Gary
    Schwendiman, eds., *Management by Japanese Systems*. New York:
    Praeger Publishers, 1982.

Hyman, Richard. "Flexible Specialization: Miracle or Myth?" in
    Hyman and Streek, eds. *New Technology and Industrial Relations*.
    Basil Blackwell, 1988.

Jacobs, George W. "Quality Circles and Japanese Management:
    Participation or Paternalism?" In Sang M. Lee and Gary
    Schwendiman, eds., *Management by Japanese Systems*. New York:
    Praeger Publishers, 1982.

Kamata, Satoshi. *Japan in the Passing Lane: An Insider's Account of
    Life in a Japanese Auto Factory*. Translated and edited by Tatsuru
    Akimoto. New York: Pantheon Books, 1973.

Kaplinsky, Raphael. "Restructuring the capitalist labour process: some
    lessons from the car industry." *Cambridge Journal of Economics*
    12 (4) (December, 1988).

Katzenstein, Peter J. *Small States in World Markets: Industrial
    Policy in Europe*. Ithaca: Cornell University Press, 1985.

Kawanishi, Hirosuke. *Enterprise Unionism in Japan*. New York: Kegan
    Paul International, 1992.

Kiyoshi, Yamamoto. "Labor-Management Relations at Nissan Motor Co., Ltd. (Datsun)." *Annals of the Institute of Social Science* No. 21. (1980).

Korpi, Walter. *The Working Class in Welfare Capitalism: Work, Unions and Politics in Sweden.* Boston: Routledge and Kegan Paul, 1978.

Mahon, Rianne. "From Fordism To ?: New Technology, Labour Markets and Unions." *Economic and Industrial Democracy* Vol. 8 (1987).

Mahon, Rianne. "From Solidaristic Wages to Solidaristic Work: A Post-Fordist Historic Compromise for Sweden?" *Economic and Industrial Democracy* Vol 12 (1991).

Marsh, Robert M. "The Difference Between Participation and Power in Japanese Factories." *Industrial and Labor Relations Review* Vol 45, No 2 (January, 1992).

Martin, Andrew. "Sweden: Industrial Democracy and Social Democratic Strategy." In G David Garson, ed., *Worker Self Management in Industry: The West European Experience.* New York: Praeger Publishers, 1977.

Martin, Andrew. "Trade Unions in Sweden: Strategic Responses to Change and Crisis." In Peter Gourevitch, Andre Martin, George Ross et al., *Unions and Economic Crisis: Britain, West Germany and Sweden.* Boston: George Allen and Unwin, 1984.

Monden, Yasuhiro. *Toyota Production System: Practical Approach to Production Management.* Atlanta: Industrial Engineering and Management Press, 1983.

Moore, Joe. "Production Control: Workers' Control in Early Postwar Japan." In E. Patricia Tsurumi, ed., *The Other Japan: Postwar Realities.* Armonk, NY: M.E. Sharpe, Inc., 1988.

Nightingale, David. "The Co-determination and Quality of Work Life Movements Compared." In Dlugos et al., eds., *Management Under Differing Value Systems.* New York: Walter de Gruyter Press, 1981.

Odaka, Konosuke, Keinosuke Ono, and Fumihiko Adachi. *The Automobile Industry in Japan: A Study of Ancillary Firm Development*. Oxford: Kinokuniya Company LTD, Oxford University Press, 1988.

Ohno, Taiichi. "How the Toyota Production was Created." In Kazuo Sato and Yasuo Hoshino, eds., *The Anatomy of Japanese Business*. Armonk, NY: ME Sharpe, Inc., 1984.

Parker, Mike and Jane Slaughter. *Choosing Sides: Unions and the Team Concept*. Boston: South End Press, 1988.

Parker, Mike. *Inside the Circle: A Union Guide to QWL*. Boston: South End Press, 1985.

Pempel, T.J. *Policy and Politics in Japan: Creative Conservatism*. Philadelphia: Temple University Press, 1982.

Piore, Michael and Charles Sabel. *The Second Industrial Divide: Possibilities for Prosperity*. New York: Basic Books, 1984.

Plowman, David H. and Bill Ford. "Employee Participation in Japan." In Ed Davis and Russel Lansbury, eds., *Democracy and Control in the Workplace*. Australia: Longman Cheshire, 1986.

Pontusson, Jonas. "Radicalism and Retreat in Swedish Social Democracy." *The New Left Review* Number 165 (Sept/Oct 1987).

Pontusson, Jonas. "The Politics of New Technology and Job Redesign: A Comparison of Volvo and British Leyland." *Economic and Industrial Democracy* Vol 11 (1990).

Sabel, Charles F. *Work and Politics: The division of labor in industry*. New York: Cambridge University Press, 1982.

Sandberg, Åke, et al. *Technological Change and Co-Determination in Sweden*. Philadelphia: Temple University Press, 1992.

Schonberger, Richard J. "Inventory Control in Japanese Industry." In Sang M. Lee and Gary Schwendiman, eds., New York: Praeger Publishers, 1982.

Schonberger, Richard. *Japanese Manufacturing Techniques: Nine Hidden Lessons in Simplicity*. New York: The Free Press, 1982.

Shimokawa, Koichi. "Product and Labour Strategies in Japan." In Tolliday and Zeitlin, eds., *The Automobile Industry and its Workers*. New York: St. Martin's Press, 1987.

Smitka, Michael J. *Competitive Ties: Subcontracting in the Japanese Automotive Industry*. New York: Columbia University Press, 1991.

Stephens, John D. *The Transition from Capitalism to Socialism*. Urbana and Chicago: University of Illinois Press, 1979.

Streeck, Wolfgang. "Industrial Relations and Industrial Change: the Restructuring of the World Automobile Industry in the 1970s and 1980s." *Economic and Industrial Democracy* Vol. 8 (1987).

Tabatoni, Pierre. "The Market Economies Tack Against the Wind: Coping with Economic Shocks 1973-1983." In Industrial Relations Research Association Series, *Industrial Relations in a Decade of Economic Change*. Illinois: Pantagraph Printing, 1985.

Taylor, Lynda King. "Worker Participation in Sweden." *Industrial and Commercial Training* (1973).

Tokunaga, Shigeyoshi. "A Marxist Interpretation of Japanese Industrial Relations, with Reference to Large Private Enterprises." In Taishiro Shirai, ed., *Contemporary Industrial Relations in Japan*. Madison: University of Wisconsin Press, 1983.

Tolliday, Steven and Jonathan Zeitlin, eds. *The Automobile Industry and its Workers: Between Fordism and Flexibility*. New York: St. Martin's Press, 1987.

Turner, Lowell. *Democracy at Work*. Ithaca: Cornell University Press, 1991.

Yakushiji, Taizo. "The Government in a Spiral Dilemma: Dynamic Policy Interventions Vis-á-Vis Auto Firms. C.1900-C.1960." In

Masahiko Aoki, ed., *The Economic Analysis of the Japanese Firm.*
New York: North-Holland, 1984.

Index